What others are saying

I first met Ian in 1994 when he came to share his testimony at Cornerstone Bromley in the suburbs of London. I was responsible for the Tv ministry which was the beginning of Christian Television in the United Kingdom. God was about to do a mighty work in reaching the British audience with the Gospel.

We as the media team recorded all the Sunday services except one, and that was Ian McCormack's testimony. Why did I not record it you might you ask? To be honest, when I read the outline and topic of what Ian was going to be sharing, I simply thought this was going to be one hooky message, so I gave the media crew the day off from filming and we sat in with the congregation.

Ian began telling his encounter of his night dive which led to him being stung by several Box Jellyfish, who are one of the deadliest creatures on the earth and without giving too much away on this almost incredible story. It wasn't long after Ian started sharing his Night Dive to Heaven account that I was very much regretting that we weren't filming his testimony.

By the time Ian was giving his account on entering the presence of our Lord, as by now he was no longer alive in the flesh and what Ian experienced had convinced me this was not a made-up story and was unlike any other NDE I had come across. Some how I needed to get this amazing encounter filmed in order to bring hope to many other dear souls.

We filmed for over an hour, but I could only include fifteen minutes of the interview in our first week's broadcast as I had already edited the other interviews into our two-hour show. Therefore, I called the CEO of the BET London Network and said that I desperately needed to buy more time on the Sunday morning in order to include the whole of Ian's testimony.

This meant that we were going to drain our funds, but I felt it was so important for the viewers to hear and see Ian that we committed to broadcasting it whatever the cost.

On the following Monday morning after our first broadcast, the CEO of the TV Station called me and said, "WHAT AN AMAZING INTERVIEW THAT WAS WITH IAN"

And he went onto say that we didn't have to pay for the extra time we booked for the Sunday and what's more, we could have every Sunday morning for free every week."

I believe this was because even the hardest of hearts could see just how genuine Ian McCormack's testimony is and there is never a better time than right now for others in the world to also know that there is a New Heaven and a New Earth coming soon as God promised in Revelation Chapter 21.

Meanwhile, now is the time for Night Dive to Heaven.

—Howard Conder, Founder of Revelation TV

I first met Ian when he was travelling in USA in the 1990s. Fourteen years after his extraordinary conversion, he could still barely control his emotions when he spoke of it. There was a deep devotion to Jesus, and a tenderness and humility about him as well as warmth and humour. So I thought I knew the man and his story! However as I began to read this book I was captivated; there was so much I didn't know about his pre-Christian days, and also the last few years too! I found the whole journey absolutely riveting. It is not only the amazing facts of his story that are so compelling, but the honesty and humility with which he tells it. He, and his beautiful wife Jane share their ups and downs with rare vulnerability that draws the reader in, becoming accessible and relatable while at the same time inspiring and encouraging us. This is a fabulous story, which has already won many to Jesus in the verbal form, and I hope and pray will win many more in its literary form.

—Wendy Virgo

I have had the joy of knowing Ian for 30 years. During these years I've heard him speak on a number of occasions and have enjoyed fellowship with him many times. The way that Ian shines the love of Jesus is a living example for everyone one of us.

Ian's testimony of how God rescued him from the fatal stings of not one but five of the deadliest jellyfish in the world is one of the most compelling you will ever read, a true story of being raised from the dead. Although not a Christian at the time, he encountered Jesus and was returned to his body—as you can imagine, with a whole new perspective!

Night Dive to Heaven has truly captured Ian's incredible afterlife encounter. While I have often heard him share it, It never gets "old" and always recalibrates me back to the perspective of eternity. Everyone should take the time to read *Night Dive to Heaven*; in its pages you will encounter the love of the Father and His heart of humility.

—Chris Gore
Minister and Author of *#Positioned and Apprehended Identity*
Orewa, New Zealand

It is with much enthusiasm that I write this endorsement of Ian's book. I have known Ian and his wife Jane for over 40 years and have been inspired by Ian's experience of death and what he saw beyond. My responsibility for Ian his been one of overseeing his life and ministry and providing him an accountability as he travelled the world relating his story. Ian is a man of excellence and integrity. He grew up in New Zealand in a loving family. His mother was woman of prayer as can be seen in the book. Her prayers and love for Ian are a huge part of his story. The book speaks of Ian's diving experiences in Mauritius were he was hit by the stings of the sea wasps. We know of them as box jellyfish. Slowly paralysis set into his body and he died an agonizing death in the local hospital. There are people alive and well in Mauritius today who were diving with Ian and witnessed his death. His description of his spirit returning to his body after his death is amazing. What he saw after dying and his experience with the reality of God is revealing and challenging for us all. Imagine meeting Jesus and then seeing heaven and hell. This would convince even the most doubting unbeliever.

Night Dive to Heaven is well written and factual to my understanding. The writer has researched well and expressed clearly a story that needed to be told. The book is a great read and I wholeheartedly endorse it.

—Denis Humphreys, Senior Pastor A/G New Zealand and ex Executive member of the Assemblies of God New Zealand

NIGHT DIVE TO HEAVEN

The Miraculous Life Changing Experience of
IAN McCORMACK
as told to Richard Drebert

EABooks Publishing
Your Partner In Publishing

Night Dive to Heaven, The Miraculous Life Changing Experience of
IAN McCORMACK as told to Richard Drebert
©2023 © Christ is Creator Ministry Inc., PO Box 34117, Indialantic Fl 32903.

All rights reserved. No part of this publication may be reproduced or transmitted in any form or by any electronic or mechanical means including photo copying, recording, or any information storage and retrieval system now known or to be invented, without permission in writing from the publisher or the author.

Scripture quotations are taken from the Holy Bible, New Living Translation (NLT) © Tyndale House Publishers.

Cover by BookDesigners.com
Cover photos from Shutterstock

ISBN: 978-1-955309-73-8

Published by Christ is Creator Ministry Inc.
In association with EA Books Publishing, a division of
Living Parables of Central Florida, Inc. a 501c3
EABooksPublishing.com

*Dedicated to my late mother
Marie McCormack.*

Her prayers and life have changed me for all Eternity. What an amazing mother, friend, and example she has been to me. Her kind, forgiving heart enabled me to navigate the most difficult times in my life.

Words can't describe the love and respect I have for her and I can't wait to see her again when I once again cross over onto eternity's shores.

*God is Light, and in Him
is no darkness at all.*
1 John 1:5

FOREWORD

Ian McCormack's story in *Night Dive to Heaven* is profoundly moving and completely credible. I believe that reading this powerful book will cause readers to ask life's ultimate questions: *Why am I here, Where did I come from, and Where am I going?*

As a retired general practitioner and anaesthetist, I have no doubt that Ian died following multiple stings from Box Jellyfish, which is one of the most venomous creatures in the world. Death from Box Jellyfish stings can occur within five minutes. Death is due to Respiratory Failure caused by paralysis of the Respiratory Center in the brain, or to direct effects on the heart causing electrical conduction disturbances and paralysis of the cardiac muscle. Patients who have been stung by Box Jellyfish frequently become unconscious before leaving the water.

In my opinion Ian McCormack sustained a cardiac arrest, due to the toxic effects of Box Jellyfish stings. A considerable time had elapsed before the antitoxin could be administered in the hospital, making the prognosis extremely poor.

Ian's account of Jesus Christ, Heaven and Hell are completely in agreement with Biblical descriptions. In fact, like all Biblical events, the truth of these events should be checked against the Scriptures, as the Bereans did in Acts 17:11. Ian became an ordained Minister in 1991 and has travelled widely all over the world speaking about his experience ever since. Ian has made it his lifetime goal to see as many people as possible end up in Heaven, rather than Hell, which is the reason for his travelling. His motive is not financial.

According to the Bible, when we die our spirit leaves our bodies.

Paul himself seems to have had a Near Death Experience after he was stoned to death by Jews from Antioch and Iconium in Acts 14:19.

The Jews were extremely angry with Paul for deserting the Sanhedrin and becoming a follower of Jesus. It is certain that Paul was stoned to death, since Paul was described as "dead", and the original Greek word, *thnéskó*, indicates that Paul was truly dead. Most Bible scholars believe that Paul was describing his own Near Death Experience when he was *"caught up into the Third Heaven"* in 2 Corinthians 12:2, which is a Biblical validation of Near Death Experiences.

Finally, Dr Luke describes the spirit of a dead 12-year-old girl returning to her body so that she came back to life. Jesus was called to see Jairus' daughter who had died, with the request that He should bring the girl back to life again. The story is recorded in Luke 8:53-55, *'They ridiculed Him knowing that she was dead but he put them all outside, took her hand and called saying, "Little girl arise". Then her spirit returned and she arose immediately".*

Ian's testimony so greatly impressed me that I co-authored three books on Near Death Experiences, and have travelled widely to many countries speaking on Near Death Experiences myself.

I sincerely hope readers are confronted with the reality of Heaven and Hell, and then ensure that own destiny in Heaven, and encourage others to do the same.

—Dr Richard Kent

Dr Richard Kent is a retired medical doctor. He has the co-authored the books *The Final Frontier*, *Beyond the Final Frontier*, and *Return from Eternity*, which include 51 near death experiences. Please visit his website www.drrichardkent.org.

HOW MY BOOK IS WRITTEN

Night Dive to Heaven is the true story of my death, my encounter with Jesus in heaven, and my return to build a fulfilling earthly life and ministry with my wife, Jane. Through our unconventional union and challenges, God has taught us the meaning of oneness and compassion.

My account is not a word-for-word transcript of events and conversations. But I have preserved the drama and feelings spanning a lifetime as accurately as I remember. Some names and places, etc., have been changed to protect the privacy of individuals.

As for meeting Jesus, the One True Light—*this* experience, and my descriptions of hell and heaven, are forged into my consciousness as though they happened yesterday. This one powerful encounter is the entire reason I continue to do what I do.

—Ian McCormack

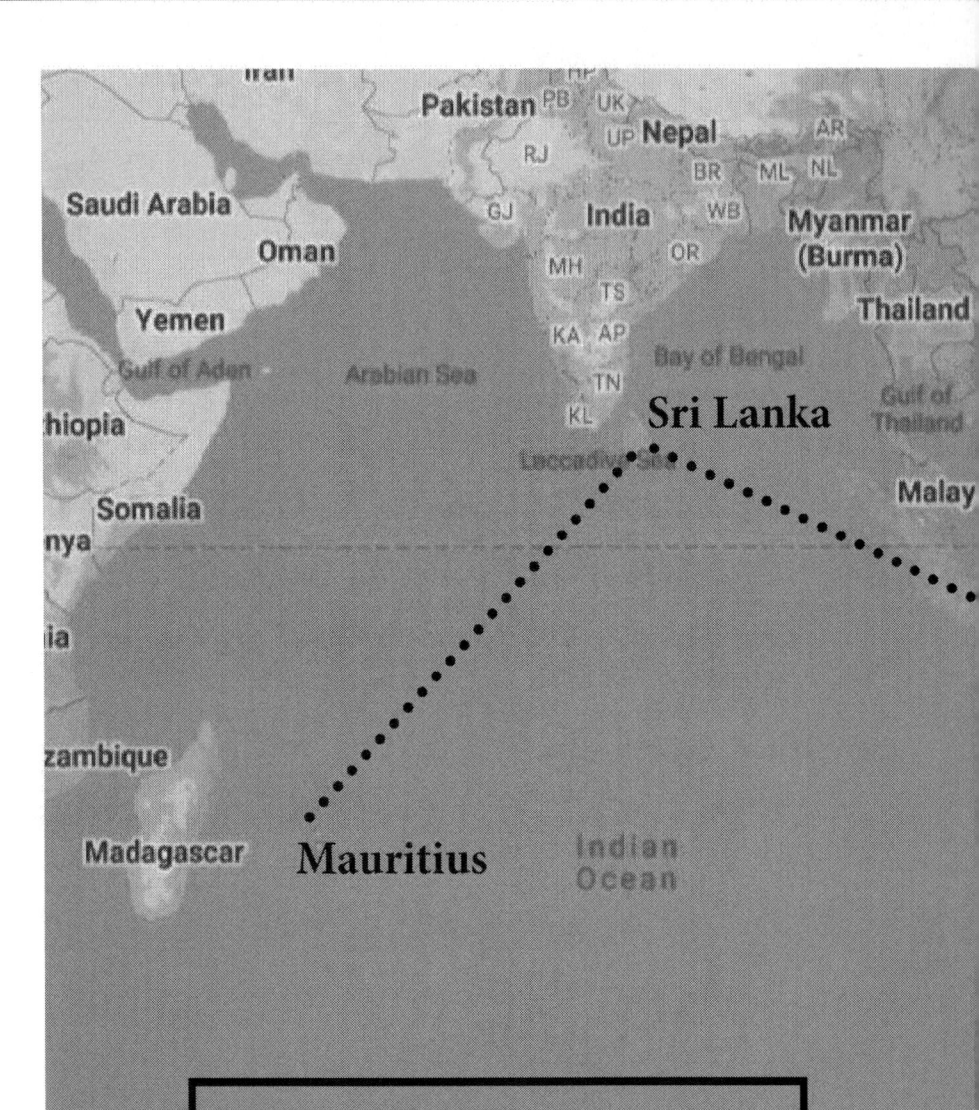

Ian's Route to Mauritius

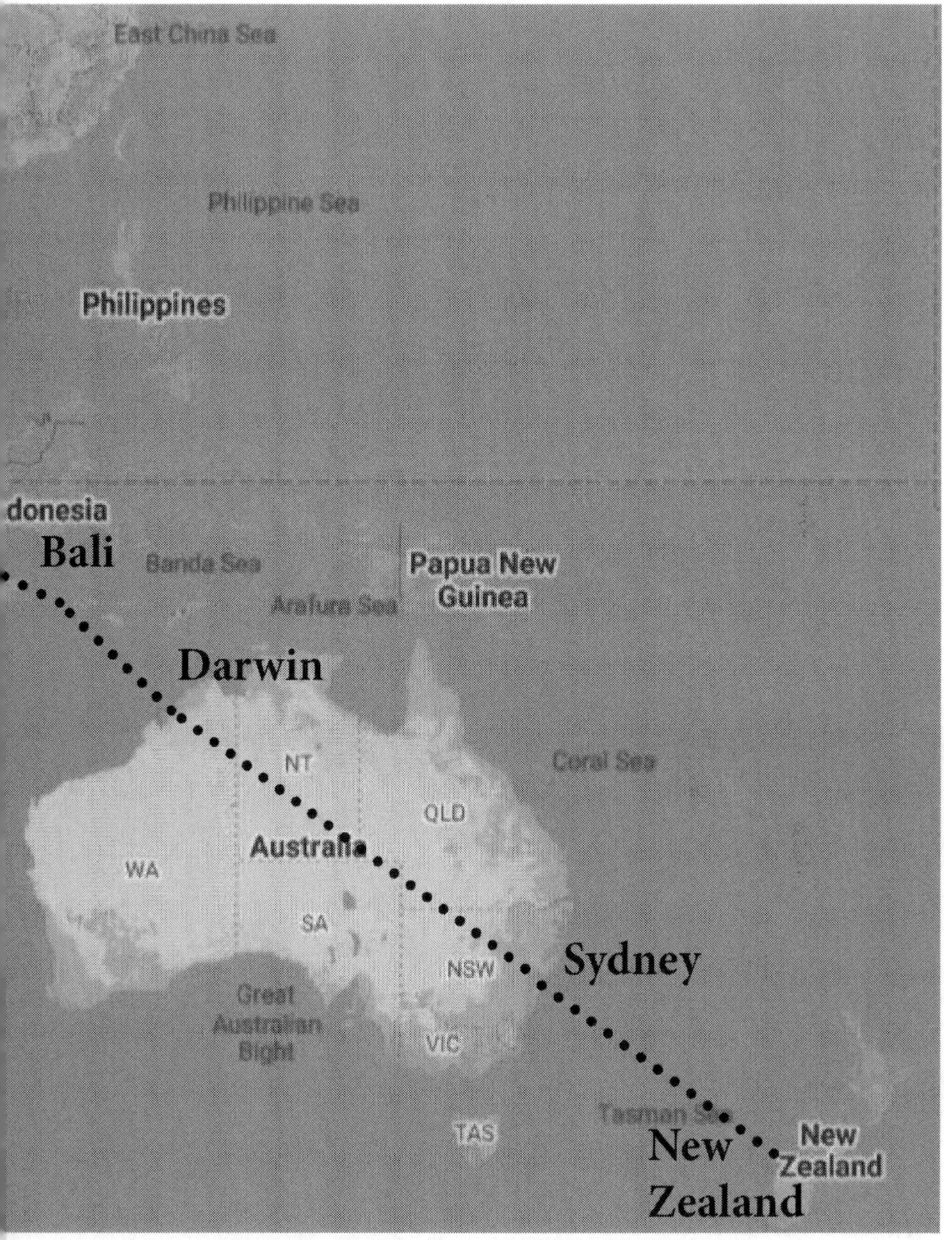

East China Sea
Philippine Sea
Philippines
donesia
Bali
Banda Sea
Arafura Sea
Papua New
Guinea
Darwin
NT
Coral Sea
QLD
Australia
WA
SA
Sydney
NSW
Great
Australian
Bight
VIC
TAS
Tasman Sea
New
Zealand
New
Zealand

INTRODUCTION

My poisoned body crumpled into a rickety wheelchair. I was feeling the venom painfully migrate through my limbs.

"I-I'm dying," I faltered. "I've been stung by *five sea wasps!* I need antitoxin…"

The old Hindu doctor studied my chart for seconds, then hurriedly shoved my wheelchair down the hall to an emergency room.

"We're going to try to save your life, son. You must try and keep your eyes open or you will die. Fight the poison!"

Understanding the gravity of the situation, a tightlipped nurse frantically plumbed for a vein. After she thrust the needle inside, my blood vessel ballooned and antitoxin struggled to move through my veins. It didn't work. Blood was scarcely trickling through my arteries, veins, and tissue. By this point, I began feeling the rhythm of my heart fading.

Another nurse filled a second hypo. Fluid spouted from the needle point, and her fingers trembled as she pinched my numb flesh. She slid the shaft in, and my collapsed vein rejected the life-saving antitoxin again.

Nurses in the room stared at one another. Paralysis claimed my limbs, but I could hear and see everything.

"Another one?" a nurse asked.

The doctor shook his head. He leaned close to my face. "Don't be afraid," he whispered gently.

Immediately, I understood that his compassionate demeanor signaled the prognosis of death.

Orderlies lifted me onto a bed.

A sense of aloneness and abandonment seized me. With all my will power, I tried to move my head, but my neck and shoulders seemed to be welded together. Only my eyelids fluttered, like moth wings. I was fighting death, but death was overpowering my paralyzed, poisoned form.

Suddenly my whole body let out a sigh, releasing all of its oxygen into the atmosphere. My battle to stay alive was over. The world went dark. Death had won.

On beaches south of the equator, signs are painted with skull and crossbones to warn tourists to avoid swimming where sea wasps have invaded the reefs. Also known as "box jellyfish" or "Chironex fleckeri," a sea wasp's poison is one of the deadliest venoms on earth. It ravages a swimmer's nervous system within a few strokes.

With its trailing tentacles, one sea wasp can inject multiple stingers from 5,000 cells into prey at nearly forty miles per hour. My death had been caused by the sting of *five* box jellyfish. Their tentacles had lashed my right arm.

Before this ill-fated night dive, I had explored coral reefs and caves fearlessly, wandering remote islands of the Indian Ocean. At 26 years old, few swimmers could match my endurance and survival skills. I had mounted thundering azure waves at home in New Zealand and surfed the most inaccessible breaks of Australia, Indonesia, South Africa, and Sri Lanka. This included the island of Mauritius, where the Creole brotherhood granted me passage to secret coves to dive at night.

I had survived all that the ocean gods could conjure before this one horrifying night, when I lay helpless and drooling in a WWII-era hospital. The hands of time were stuck in muck—and only once before had I felt so vulnerable.

I was a teenager when it happened the first time. The ocean flung me about like an empty seashell, and the sands of time ceased falling through the hourglass. Believing I was immortal, I had underestimated the brutality of a South Seas cyclone.

Now my body lay in an island hospital where I was about to come face to face with the all-powerful Creator whom I had dismissed my entire life. This one divine encounter completely changed the entire course of my life.

So had I really been abandoned? Quite the opposite…

CHAPTER 1

SLAP OF MORTALITY

Wahine

Most New Zealanders that I know possess an aversion to violence and have an avid desire for peace for our families. We haven't forgotten our brave soldiers who died at Gallipoli in World War I, nor the Kiwi blood spilled in World War II. And sailing back to earlier decades, we're still troubled over the Maori Wars in New Zealand when we fought over territory and resources.

National tragedies, too, have left scars.

In a narrow channel between New Zealand's North and South Islands, a tropical cyclone called Giselle wreaked havoc upon the inter-island ferry *Wahine*. Driven by 160 mph winds, the ferry struck Barrett Reef in Wellington Harbor. The *Wahine* capsized, and fifty-one souls drowned—and our island nation mourned.

Those of us from New Zealand call spiraling storms that carry high tropical winds *cyclones*. Cyclones swirl in a counterclockwise direction and are similar to hurricanes that swirl in a clockwise direction.

For months after the *Wahine* maritime disaster, cyclones continued to ravage our shores. It was during one of these storms that a brash teenager and a few of his mates challenged the fury of the tempest.

With my six-foot six-inch single fin surfboard, I kicked off my *jandals* (Kiwi for sandals) on the white sands of Waihi Beach, not far from my family's *bach* (a Kiwi summer home). At the tail end of the '60s, our bach wasn't much more than two quarter-acre sections with old structures that my father had purchased before I was born. On one section he remodeled the buildings, and in later years he built my grandparents (his dad and mum) a home on the other.

My brother, sister, Mum and I followed Dad and his vocation as a teacher to various towns on the North Island, but our bach was the family's safe harbor. It was our permanent port of call. For years we collected drinking water into rain barrels from roof runoff, and made use of a "long drop" (outhouse), until Dad could afford to install indoor plumbing.

As a child, I couldn't wait to anchor at our bach each summer. The bach was where I stowed my surfboard, wetsuit, and snorkeling gear for all of my adventures.

"No worries, mate!"

The wind nearly ripped my surfboard from my hands, and I splashed into the frothy sea, glancing back at my part-Maori surfing mate, Butch. He and other spectators waited near my dad's Austin Cambridge that I had driven to the beach. My audience watched me slam my board onto a wave and attack the first swell as it raised me on its palm. It dumped me into a trough, then elevated my board high and slapped me down again.

Adrenaline pumped through my body as I conquered the powerful current. I felt invincible. I had been awarded the Bronze Medallion from, and held membership with, the Royal Life Saving Society. My instructor at Rotorua's Blue Baths had been pressing me to swim competitively.

I wasn't just a "good" swimmer. I demonstrated endurance and speed that rivaled the best young athletes in New Zealand, many who were much older than me. And though I loved snatching victory from other swimmers in a pool, the lure of ocean surf had become my deep and abiding addiction. The wondrous varieties in surfing "breaks" captivated me, and I often ditched swim practice (mandated twice a day, seven days a week) to drive my board through a tube. I longed to own every break in Waihi Beach, including the sloppy giants thundering toward the borrowed Austin parked safely inland, today.

A few other crazy boarders like me paddled into the white lather, but the only "companions" close enough for me to see were shards of driftwood ground up from the storm. With all my strength, I set a course for a wave where I could line up and gain my stance in a curl.

At the top of a swell, I spotted what seemed to be the cyclone's whirling eye, and with adolescent pride I defied Nature—or Whomever provoked the sea to fury.

On my knees, and I was up—spreading arms like an eagle, planting right foot before the left, and feeling the board beneath me surge and groan. I rushed into an empty pocket, and it became a tube—for an instant—until the roof collapsed. Fingers of forceful froth yanked my board from under my feet, and a herd of whitecaps trampled me.

I was airborne for seconds, until I slammed into what felt like a concrete wall. Waves piled on top of me, pounding me deeper and deeper. I sucked in a single shallow breath before submerging, and I held it in my lungs, hoping that the ankle rope attached to my board would hold. Its buoyancy was my lifeline.

The sea entombed me.

A thought about sailors who had perished here floated inside my head, and then another unexpected thought surfaced: *Who is master of your destiny now, Ian? Are you invincible?*

I opened my eyes, reaching for equilibrium, but ocean spume drowned my senses. My limbs grew heavy, and I experienced utter helplessness for the first time. I was disoriented.

Which way is up? Where is down?

I flailed one direction but realized I was swimming into a cave of darkness—and paddled back. I stroked again a different way and broke the surface for the space of one breath, before waves drove me down again.

It felt like I had been dropped into a massive washing machine. My lungs were about ready to surrender when light grabbed my attention. I clawed my way to it, and thankfully, it wasn't my imagination. I broke the surface long enough to inhale air thinking, *Wow! That was close...*

Instantly the taunting sea pounded away my relief one more time, before waves spewed me onto the beach. Gasping and coughing, the strange feeling of timelessness vanished as I lay there battered by the sea.

What was that all about?

It was my first slap of mortality on the way to manhood. I realized that I wasn't immune to dying after all. It took some time for my cockiness to return, but it did—as inevitably as a crab regrows a claw.

KIWI HERITAGE

Blame Irish DNA for my audacity. My family roots grow from the Hill of Tara, where ancient kings of Ireland took their oaths. Distant relatives still live in County Cork, where my kin laid medieval stones to build Blarney Castle. Our McCormack family coat of arms tells a story of Gaelic charioteers—with symbols describing the warriors' cry of: *No Fear!*

Branches of our clan inhabited Scotland and England before sailing for New Zealand, bringing with them expertise in farming and a bold disposition (this was on Colin Neville McCormack's—my father's—side of the family).

Viking blood flows through our McCormack veins, and my connection to the sea and the challenge to "discover" still dogs my flesh. And though some admirable qualities, like courage, may have been carried in bloodline and traditions, my father's kin possessed little more than respect for religion and God.

My mum's relations, too, were adventurers. They sailed from Great Britain to New Zealand before the Maori Wars of the mid-1800s. Stories of hiding children in water barrels to save them from Maori warriors have been told and retold for at least three generations. My hardy New Zealand ancestors on Mum's side of the family were some of the original Kiwis who cleared land for pasture and turned soil for crops.

My mum's father, my Grandfather Bethune, died when Mum was a teenager, leaving my Mum to help her mother run the "dairy" (a small grocery store in Kiwi-speak) instead of finishing school. My Grandmother Bethune was known to be a spiritualist, and I was six years old when she received pennies on her eyes. I was considered too young to see her body in repose. She died from multiple sclerosis.

Countering Grandmother Bethune's psychic influence, my God-fearing Great Grandmother Nan, on my father's side, led her family into the Anglican (Church of England) faith and traditions. In the months before marrying my father, Nan's Christian example inspired my mother, Marie, to become a Christ follower, too.

Decades later, my mother's Christian influence had so intertwined with my life, that in my darkest moment of desperation, her words provoked me to reverse a decision that altered my future forever.

My father was reared by a staunch military man, my grandfather Arthur McCormack. Grandfather had served in the Gallipoli campaign in Turkey and at the Battle of Somme in France. World War I had jolted New Zealanders to a global awareness as they watched our Kiwi boys march into some of the bloodiest battles in modern history.

Grandfather Arthur McCormack

Grandfather Arthur was one of the most influential men in my life. He served as an RSM (Regimental Sergeant Major), responsible for advising commanders and disciplining noncommissioned subordinates. When WWI devolved into WWII, Sergeant Major McCormack fought with New Zealanders against Ervin Rommel in North Africa.

After his military discharge, Grandfather settled in Waihi Township and poured his energies into seeking gold at the Waihi mines for a time, before venturing into various other occupations. His restlessness infected others in our family too. I have a few uncles, aunts, and cousins who have sailed, flown, or marched to the military drums as well.

Nazi bayonets, German Lugers, ceremonial swords, and medals from vanquished SS officers occupied a corner of my grandfather's garage. My hero's war relics reminded my family of his personal battle to keep New Zealand free of tyranny. His Celtic fortitude has summoned me to search for my own purpose in life as well.

Grandfather McCormack never staked a claim on a particular career, and he often left one job for another. He wore the boots of a wayfaring soldier, unattached to a permanent dwelling. The war had taken its toll on his mind, and he empathized with veterans he knew who carried the crushing weight of memories.

When soldiers disembarked from troopships at New Zealand ports, they faced communities that could not understand the dread of dying or being maimed—but Grandfather understood. He helped form an ex-combatants' club (the RSA) that catered to the needs of veterans. His fulfillment came from building a community bowling green where veterans could meet and talk about their service.

Another branch of his ambition included running a boardinghouse (motel) and a "dairy" (small convenience store). But of all the enterprises my grandfather pioneered in his life, he seized upon one adventure that still impacts generations of McCormacks.

Arthur married his sweetheart, my Grandmother Ethel. The story goes, that during the months that my father courted my mum, over tea and biscuits my Great Grandmother Nan poured God's word into Mum's seeking heart. As long as she lived, God used my great grandmother to inspire my mother and others to faith in God.

My Great Grandmother's traditional Anglican affinity established a framework of tradition from which some in my family have committed their lives to Christ.

But for me...I chose to go my own way.

WOP WOPS

Unlike his brother and sister, Dad decided to teach school rather than pursue a military career, although he did inherit a soldier's cadence of discipline exemplified by his father, Sergeant Major McCormack. Blame my dad for my love of *wop wops* (Kiwi-speak for wilderness). One of his first appointments after teacher's training landed Mum, my brother, my sister, and me in a rural community called Ngutunui, at the edge of native New Zealand woodlands—paradise for a boy.

My exciting boyhood frontier extended from our three-bedroom house with a quarter-acre garden to surrounding farms with poultry, sheep, goats, horses, and dairy stock. Beyond the farmers' fields lay the native bush—my father's tramping ground, where he schooled me in backwoods survival and how to place a bullet in a deer's heart. Together we found a father-son connection, where wild boar and red deer contributed to *tucker* (Kiwi for food) at our table.

My father taught the Ngutunui farmers' kids at a "two-teacher" state school. It was on the same property as our modest home, where Mum cared for our family of five. My younger brother, Neil, and my older sister, Sharon, also attended the school where Dad taught.

The school and farms around us appeared to be gouged out of the wop wops. The forest—inhabited by not a single indigenous predator (like snakes or bears)—sheltered farm families from the cultural upheavals drifting to New Zealand from Great Britain and America. In the early '60s, few Ngutunui families owned televisions. This eliminated any sedentary habits of television watching and offered them the freedom of exploration and adventure awaiting them in the wild outdoors.

On weekends and after school, McCormack kids ran wild, like foals on a morning romp. Mum, a quiet, thoughtful woman in her late twenties with snapping blue eyes and blonde hair, held tightly to the tradition of deference to my father. Dad, at an imposing six-foot-three with penetrating dark eyes and brown hair, kept a regimented schedule, satisfying the state while keeping an eye out for more lucrative teaching positions.

Most Ngutunui farmers pastured sheep and sheared wool for profit. Dairy families emptied their sweet bovine labor into a mobile tanker mornings and evenings. Almost everyone had milk to drink, no matter how well-heeled or poor.

Three years of boyhood adventures at Ngutunui flew by, and Dad found a better position at Rotorua. Graduating from Ardmore Teachers Training College was finally paying off for Dad.

ROTORUA

"Ian! Grab his hocks, lad!"

Our pig dogs held the three-hundred-pound boar by jowl and nose, and I slogged through a thicket to reach the murky wallow. It was deeper than I thought, and pig stench besieged me. I gripped the boar's hind legs, and pig poo splattered my face and chest. Mud poured over the top of my gumboots, and the boar slashed at our dogs with jutting tusks. I held on for dear life as my father plunged his knife blade into the hog's vitals.

Dad and I hauled our "Captain Cooker" home in filthy triumph. In the 1700s, the famed Captain Cook had set loose porkies into the wilds of New Zealand, where they thrive to this day.

Hunting with my father paved my way to manhood, whether stalking boars with nothing but a knife, or bringing down a buck to fill our tucker bag for Mum. We ate what we killed like our ancestors did, and like my Maori bros who lived outside of our new town—Rotorua.

The native bush lay within minutes of Rotorua, so tramping with Dad on a weekend became our seasonal ritual. Living in Rotorua for nine years, locked in my McCormack pride as I came of age in an urban environment with schools, movie houses, and churches. From Rotorua, a world-renowned tourist town, I launched my life-long quest for adventure.

In remote Ngutunui, Mum had done her best to engraft the Christian faith in her children. She had scavenged Christian literature from neighbors or ordered it by mail. She read Bible stories to us too. But by the time I was an early teen at Rotorua Boys School, religion had become little more than background noise, like flocks of tui birds—ever present, but ignored.

With little help from my father—except to accompany us to the Anglican Church on Sundays—Mum renewed her battle to bring her children to Jesus, while I concentrated on discovering friendships and challenges beyond the family. (Mum's faith may have felt more pivotal in my life, had she shared her most cherished moment after her mother died. It wasn't until an impromptu conversation at my confirmation years later that she told me about it).

From the mid-1800s, Rotorua had been a playground for world travelers to loll in therapy pools and watch theatrical geysers perform around pristine Lake Rotorua and sixteen other lakes in the neighborhood. And now Rotorua was *my* playground.

The kid whom I chose to be my lifetime bro was a Celt too. Jack was from a related clan in County Cork, Ireland. Our ancestors likely handed stones and mortar to one another building Blarney Castle. Together, with a couple other rowdy Celts, we biked and built forts on the banks of Lake Rotorua, where Maori and British soldiers had battled over land and sovereignty in 1860.

Dad hit his professional stride while teaching at Rotorua, leading to his advancement as principal in years to come. Mum's gift as a teacher bloomed too, and her fruitful ministry as a mentor for children with learning disabilities endured long after she left Rotorua.

My brother, Neil, and my sister, Sharon, remained true to the McCormack tradition and prepared for careers—while I fought against a rising inner tide. To tamp down my craving for risky behavior, I threw myself into school sports like rugby, cricket, and competitive swimming. And though I excelled in sports, I chafed at the routines—especially my demanding seven-day-a-week swimming regimen. Unlike my other mates in swimming togs, the coach failed to ignite a desire in me to win an Olympic medal for New Zealand.

LICENSED TO STRAY

In my teenage season at Rotorua, I experienced a sea change in body, mind, and heart. By thirteen, I had sprouted to nearly six feet, and a quirky smile belied my serious nature. My blue eyes invited competition—especially with myself.

At this crucial age, Mum and Dad aspired for my confirmation into the Anglican Church, a religious milestone for all McCormacks. I certainly wasn't against it. I had been sprinkled as a tot, and I figured that a priest's validation couldn't hurt my chance at landing in heaven when I was an old codger like Grandfather. Public affirmation would stamp my ticket and give Mum peace of mind too.

So, there I was, dressed in my Sunday best. Although I wished I were on my surfboard, instead I stood in front of the frilly-robed bishop with a funny hat. His cold hand mussed my hair as he mumbled about a Holy "Ghost" who would help me live right.

The bishop seemed to think that God owned my future, and it confused me. Seldom did I "pray" to the Man Upstairs, and he never spoke to me. And what about this "ghost" that religious people talked about? How could a creepy apparition be friendly and helpful to me?

After my first communion, Mum wiped her nose with a dainty kerchief, and Dad nodded to me like he'd finished scoring a stack of math tests. My little brother yawned, loud enough for Sharon to give him an elbow. When the bishop closed the service, Dad, my brother, and my sister bolted for the exit like uncaged possums.

Well-wishers stood around chatting in the parking lot, when it struck me—perhaps my father knew more about religion than he let on. He hid his thoughts on the subject, and he seldom expressed emotion. And he professed to be Presbyterian, which sounded impressive to me.

I can't recall Dad ever saying, "I love you, son," but he expressed his regard in other ways. He never missed my rugby games, and he rousted me out of bed for most of his hunting trips. Mum, on the other hand, encouraged me verbally, and didn't feel duty-bound to pick apart my athletic performances, like my father did.

"Dad," I said, "have you ever heard God speak to you?"

Dad frowned and glanced around for Mum, who wasn't anywhere to be found. He took a few moments to cast his line for an answer.

"Nah," he said, "some people think they've heard him, but they're a bit wacked."

We shared a moment of silence, and I think he sensed that I stood at crossroads in my life.

"Ian, you be a good boy and don't buck the system, and maybe someday you'll make it up there, eh?" He glanced heavenward, and my eyes followed his.

We parted company then. He strode off to the car, and I found Mum standing outside the church, talking with the vicar. He shook my hand warmly.

"I have a kinda big question . . . Mum?" I said.

I took a deep breath, and she squeezed my arm to encourage me. It was an emotional day for Mum.

"Have you ever heard God speak to you?" I asked.

The vicar's bushy eyebrows lifted ever so slightly. Mum hesitated. She knew how her story could tarnish the stoic McCormack family image, but she didn't hold back.

"Yes, Son, I have heard God speak to me."

And that was enough mystical talk for her priest, who gathered up his robe and excused himself.

He hasn't ever heard God speak to him—like Dad, I guessed. *But why is this the first time I've heard about Mum's experience?*

"How come you've never told me this before?" I asked. "*My* prayers hit the ceiling, and it's like no one is listening. When did God speak to *you*?"

My blue eyes searched Mum's, and her voice trembled as she related the event that changed her life forever.

"When you were a toddler, you may not remember, but my mum, Grandmother Bethune, had a terrible accident. A Jersey bull ran out in front of her car, and she couldn't stop in time. An ambulance rushed your grandmother to the hospital, and when they examined her, they discovered that she had multiple sclerosis. A few years later, she died a painful death from the disease."

"I remember her dying, Mum. I didn't get to go to the funeral . . . "

"Ian, I was so broken-hearted. I didn't know what to do! I had no one to turn to and . . . "

I grabbed my mother's hand and interrupted, "But Mum, you had us, didn't you? You could have talked to us…"

Mum shook her head, unearthing memories that she would rather have left buried. "No, Son. I had too much grief. I'd lost my father as a child. Now my mum. I felt abandoned. *Alone*."

At thirteen, I could not fathom what it meant to feel abandoned. That would come later in my life.

Mum continued in a low voice. "I was in the bedroom one night, Ian, and I told God, 'If you are real, please show yourself to me. I need you to speak to me, God!'"

The words caught in her throat. Tears began to flow, but strangely, her emotions didn't touch me.

"God answered me, Ian! He spoke to me, and I saw his son, Jesus!"

Trying to digest her words, I asked grimly, "Then, does a person have to go through a tragedy in life in order for God to speak to them?"

It didn't seem fair or reasonable to me.

"No, Ian," Mum said with a smile in her voice. "But people are by nature very proud. For some of us, only a tragedy will bring them to the place of desperation, and in that moment of anguish, they see their need for Jesus. That's when they will cry out for God—like I did."

It was a lot to take in. I came back to earth with a declaration that would haunt me for years. "Mum, I haven't done anything wrong. I'm not proud . . . "

Mum stared at me with profound empathy, and at the time I didn't know why. "We all have done things that are wrong, Ian," she said sadly.

Everything Mum was saying *felt* disagreeable. Uncomfortable. Like drawing my hand against a deer pelt the wrong direction. I remembered the Ten Commandments and wondered if I had broken any—lately. I didn't think so. And now seemed like the perfect time to confess what my confirmation *really* meant to me. I gathered up my courage.

"Ya know, none of my friends go to church, Mum. I'm the only one. And I have never once heard God say anything to me, so I don't know if he's even real."

I chose my words carefully. "Is it all right for me to stop coming to church? My friends and I could do fun stuff on Sundays, you know, like surfing. They all go places on Sundays, and they want me to come."

There! I'd said it!

I had been practicing it in my head for weeks—and Mum didn't seem the least bit surprised.

"Your Dad and I have been talking about this. I won't force my beliefs on you, Son. So, if you don't come with us anymore, it's okay. You're old enough to make that choice."

Choice. On the day of my confirmation in the Anglican Church, I walked away from God and into the hippie counterculture that loomed before me like an open pit mine. Mum watched me go—and so began many years of a mother's pleading to God for a son's salvation.

Mum burst into tears, like I'd broken her heart in two.

"What's wrong? What did I do? Mum?"

She folded up a wad of tissues. "Ian," she said, "I don't know if you can learn anything from my life, but if so, remember this: No matter what you do, or how far from God you find yourself... if you call out to Jesus in your heart, he will hear you. He will forgive you, Son." Then she added seriously, "Do you understand what I am saying?"

I felt like a five-year-old perching on Mum's lap after a scolding. "Yes, Mum. You are saying that no matter what I do wrong, and no matter how far I go from God, if I call out to Him from my heart, he'll forgive me."

We stood together then, and she buried her face in my shoulder. "Remember this, Ian. If nothing else." She said it through tears, and her words remain engraved on my soul to this day.

It wasn't long after my confirmation that I challenged the sea during a cyclone—and found my life hanging by a thread. The sea had spat me onto the beach where I had stooped against wind-driven sand to join friends joshing at Dad's old Austin.

I didn't let on to my bros how shaken I was. For the first time, swimming in my bountiful, welcoming sea, I had been as helpless as a minnow. The sea had held me under until I nearly drowned, and the whole confusing episode—so close to my mother's revelation—confused me.

And once again I asked myself, *Man! What is this all about? What is the truth?*

HIPPIE INVASION

An "assault" upon our Kiwi culture during the '60s changed New Zealand forever. Seductive anti-establishment ideas replaced foundational beliefs and traditions handed down from previous generations. By the '70s, the Woodstock counterculture had infiltrated our homes, schools, and teen hangouts. A plague of New Age philosophies spread through television and thousands of visiting tourists, dressed in bell-bottoms, moo-moos, and skimpy togs.

We teenagers showed solidarity with our hippie bros in the British Isles and America by decorating car windows and surfboards with peace decals, and by soaking in music from drug-tainted bands like the Beatles, Santana, and Pink Floyd. My devil-may-care attitude blended well with the "no boundaries" philosophy of the counterculture.

Young men in their twenties had lost all inhibitions, along with their razors. They cruised on beaches before surfing our Waihi Beach breaks, and at bonfires they shared marijuana joints while describing Bali, Singapore, and Sri Lanka. There, a hippie could score heaps of illegal drugs. Those who had traveled Asia claimed that psychedelic "herbs" like magic mushrooms helped them unlock their consciousness to a deeper spiritual understanding.

Authors like mystic Carlos Castaneda opened *my* teenage mind to pathways of psychedelics and psychic awareness. His shamanistic philosophy hooked my curiosity, but at the time, I limited my exploration to a few beers and joints when socializing.

I had set an appointment with a Royal New Zealand Air Force recruiter and expected to become a maritime pilot. I was required to test negative for drugs, and upon entry to their training program, keep a clear head as a pilot.

But a "perfect storm" made landfall in my personal life when I visited the Air Force enlistment officer.

After an eye exam, he matter-of-factly informed me, "When you graduate high school, Mr. McCormack, we can employ you as an airfield technician. But it's your eyes, Son. They aren't up to the Air Force standard for flying."

My dreams of piloting a Skyhawk over New Zealand crashed, and no other Air Force position excited me. I back-paddled away from a military career.

So, what should a McCormack do next? My little brother had set a trajectory for the New Zealand Army, and my sister studied nursing. But I needed a vocation that afforded me freedom to surf and travel.

Our nation was known as an agricultural juggernaut, supplying Europe with mutton, lumber, dairy products, and beef. I fondly remembered my sojourn in farm country as a gangly six-year-old. I had been the Ngutunui's adopted "farmers' son" among the dairymen and shepherds of the community.

My ancestors had been New Zealand's first farmers, and my McCormack hands easily fit to plow handles. It seemed natural to aim for a career that gave me latitude to roam while helping farmers improve crop yields and increase livestock production. And agricultural sciences easily harmonized with my bond to forests and wildlife.

New Zealand's most prestigious agricultural institution, Lincoln College, near Christchurch, accepted me as a university student—and all I had to do was survive a last reckless year before graduating high school.

As a youth, I overlooked how God orchestrated setbacks in my life—like grounding my dream of piloting Skyhawks. Some interventions were as obvious as rescuing me from a cyclone's grip. Others affected the lives of my friends too . . .

COFFIN ON WHEELS

Our Fiat looked like a stubby-nosed cat with big eyes and a sunroof. Jack, my fellow Celt, and a couple other bros from Rotorua piled in for a joyride, egging me on to drive faster as I spun around corners. We hummed along a forest road where log trucks claimed the thoroughfare as their own, usually without argument. Their unwieldy forty-foot trailers held stacks of white pine chained to iron forks, and drivers used every inch of the "metal" road. When they negotiated downhill curves, truckers applied air brakes that rumbled like a series of thunderclaps.

After a few beers I fancied myself as adept at driving as Auckland racing icon, Bruce McClaren (deceased while testing a prototype in 1970).

I stood on the gas petal, steering carelessly, my head sticking out of the sunroof like a periscope on a sub.

How my head eluded being crushed when the Fiat rolled over again and again, I didn't understand at the time. But somehow all of us "pickled" boys survived the car's erratic tumbling. At last, our Fiat simmered on its top in the middle of the road like an upended turtle, and we dizzily crawled out of its belly, laughing at our predicament.

It seemed to me that my personal hourglass of life had (once again) ceased to drop a single grain of sand as the Fiat floundered to its top. We had rolled four times while I swam in an ocean of timelessness—the way I did during my foolish duel with the cyclone. It wasn't until the Fiat stopped rolling that I emerged from a strange time warp.

During our befuddled reflection, counting our scrapes and bruises, I shushed my friends.

Air brakes!

A sharp curve hid what we knew would be bloody carnage in a few seconds. Scrambling to turn the Fiat right side up, we shoved it onto the gravel shoulder in time for a swearing truck driver to slide past with his load of logs. His air horn screamed at us as he sped out of sight.

We scrunched back into our coffin on wheels and drove it back to Rotorua.

At 18 years old, I felt the greatest fulfillment when I surfed or dived, and I obsessed about traveling to beaches beyond New Zealand. I had counted coup on every break within a hundred miles of our Waihi Beach house, and I yearned to explore the islands of the Indian Ocean. A passion to travel nagged at me, and every wave challenged me with: *There are bigger and more magnificent breaks to conquer, Ian. Find them.*

My homeland of New Zealand was shrinking in size and excitement, while my university at Christchurch on the South Island opened the grandest panorama of worldly experiences a naïve surfer kid could fathom. I finally felt untethered from family and morals, and I dived in.

CHAPTER 2

RIPTIDE

Lincoln

The bell chimed a dignified welcome from the tower at Ivey Hall when I arrived at Lincoln University. A seasoned upperclassman shook my hand. He escorted me along a pathway through imposing gothic architecture. Lincoln was New Zealand's old-world bastion of stability from which a "village" of lively students launched agricultural careers. I stuffed my duffle bag and surfboard into assigned quarters at the Halls of Residence, ignoring its scant elbowroom.

In the following weeks, I immersed myself in Lincoln's scholastic routines—and joined the local Lincoln rugby team as well. At tryouts, my new rugby coach and teammates appreciated my craving to win at all costs and placed me in the bruising "loose forward" position. After sprawling at a desk for hours listening to lectures on crop yields and plant sciences, I desperately needed a contact sport to wrestle down pent-up aggression. My surfboard branded me as a peculiar bloke to my fellow classmates, even though my ambition to graduate with an agricultural degree matched their own.

I ached to challenge the waves pounding the South Island shoreline an hour or so away. The sea's overtures never abated. Like a Celtic siren, its magnetic force continued to summon me with its lure of lustful adrenaline that only a surfer would understand.

To assuage the pain of trading my surfboard for books on agronomy, I pursued a scuba diving certification along with my studies. With air tanks, I learned to dive far beneath restrictive snorkeling depths.

Most of us LU students were barely out of our teens and reveled in living away from home for the first time. Like noisy gulls, our minds awakened to racial and social injustice, as well as environmental concerns.

Several of my friends came from prominent New Zealand farming dynasties and plowed rigid furrows of family expectations. I had no legacy of croplands waiting for me back home, but my father's expectations tangled with my emotions like pesky vines. I hoped to uproot his regimented influence once and for all.

At college, I marveled at the new horizons stretching before me. I wanted to change the world! At parties and gatherings, I joined with students as we shared frustrations over how the "establishment" (decision-makers in governments) ravaged the environment and hoarded wealth that could provide food to third-world nations.

Whenever a professing Christian fell into my crosshairs, I turned a polite discussion about God into a bloody battle. I had convinced myself that life evolved from primordial soup, and I tested my atheism on every person I met. I found a morbid satisfaction in dismantling a young Christian's faith with my passionate logic.

Our professors (one had a breed of sheep named after him) fed my hungry intellect to the gills. My teachers armed me with the latest agricultural technology to boost a greater yield of grains per acre. Among experts, I experimented with types of silage to produce healthier dairy stock. My farming passion thrived like spring gardens as I learned the secrets of enriching soils.

Outside the lecture halls, croplands and greenhouses dominated the countryside. And just nine miles from Lincoln lay historic Christchurch, the largest city in the South Island, and the oldest in New Zealand. I earned college credit for the hours that I worked for wages, helping in milking sheds, feeding stock, and running equipment at farms all over the region.

Diving adventures filled my weekend calendar, staged from Christchurch. Sometimes my recreation included encounters with orcas, Hector's Dolphins, and yellow-eyed penguins at marine reserves like Flea Bay and Lynch Reef.

Few of my college friends owned surfboards or diving equipment. So, after classes, I drove to the beach and often surfed alone. I was as content with the solitude as a lighthouse keeper. It was during these solo expeditions that an uneasy tide carried troubling questions to my fertile mind.

As a budding atheist, I lived in a God-free zone with boundaries that I alone controlled. I rejected my mother's Anglican religion, still labeling her faith as a crutch for old ladies and children.

My quest for knowledge and fulfillment felt bottomless, and it always led me back to the comfort I experienced at sea. Diving among sharks and challenging deadly surf awakened the metaphysical side of Ian McCormack. Gambling with life and limb interrupted the gnawing reflections about my destiny. I felt rebelliously alive when the stakes were highest.

I worshiped the sea and reverenced flora and fauna birthed by Mother Earth (for lack of a better title). My interpretations of "good" and "evil" floated in a fog of self-gratification—though my memory of one supernatural event as a child left me confused...

My father had moved us to the Ngutunui, Waikato region, and my grandparents lived at Waihi Beach. One night I awoke, frozen in fear. Beside my bed, "someone" stood staring down at me. It appeared to be my Grandfather Arthur, whom I knew loved me dearly, yet this "person" seemed menacing. Its demeanor clutched at my soul. It beckoned me to yield to its power, requesting an entrance "into" my body...

Then, as suddenly as the apparition filled space, it evaporated.

The following morning, I was grief stricken and alarmed when my mum told me that Grandfather Arthur had died that night. He was irreplaceable in my life. Two world wars had ravaged his mind, but he had always cleared his personal field of battle to be a grandson's best friend.

Traditional Māoris believe that their deceased ancestors hover around the living. Maori families build spirit houses and hang pictures of dead relatives to whom they offer prayers for guidance.

But even as a frightened child, I judged *my* dark visitor's intentions as malicious, and I knew that it was *not* my beloved grandfather.

For reasons I could never fathom, I wasn't allowed to attend Grandfather Arthur's funeral, and my disturbing visitor left a calling card to mark the occasion—I suffered vulgar dreams that troubled my sleep for years thereafter.

By the time I reached my teens, I had shrugged off this encounter as a childish nightmare. In fact, I believed that "evil" was a word staked to any activity that "Christians" didn't like. I attached no "personality" (like the devil or demons) to acts of depravity or perversion.

By college, my uncompromising atheism had gradually morphed into a transcendental agnosticism—I couldn't ignore that an unseen world existed alongside my own. And if mysterious forces ruled nature and intruded upon humanity, I wanted to study and understand them.

Books by mystic Carlos Castaneda and other freethinkers inspired me to research the "use" of natural herbs to open occult portals, and I connected with other students who were searching for ethereal dimensions beyond our present world.

At parties, I met horticulture students whose curiosity meshed with my own. They competed with one another in growing strains of marijuana in secluded forest glens, and I experienced my first real "high" with a draft-dodging American from Chicago. He had stuffed hashish in a pipe and told me it was pot.

After moving from the Halls of Residence, I spent a few contentious months with my uncle Bruce, who lived minutes from Lincoln. Bruce was my father's eldest brother and set rigid rules for the privilege of "bivouacking" (crashing) at his home. He was a regimental sergeant major with the New Zealand Army, and we didn't see eye-to-eye regarding my time management.

To experience unfettered freedom from authority, I rented a farmhouse with other students and pursued a lifestyle that would have shocked my family had they known about it. A riptide of experimentation held me in its grip, from which I had no desire to escape.

SOARING HIGH

A seagull's aerial acrobatics had always impressed me. At the same time, a gull's squabbling over crab legs or fish heads reminded me of human jealousy and greed...

A friend introduced me to a fictional novella written from the perspective of a rebellious seagull. The vivid, animistic story about a seabird described my own inner struggle and my path in seeking contentment:

Jonathan Livingston Seagull refused to conform to his feathered society and attained happiness through personal ambition. Soon he was cast out of his flock, but unexpectedly discovered fulfillment in achieving technical aerial levels of flight alone.

Jonathan gains mystical power and crosses supernatural thresholds. He meets other seagulls like himself who have transcended the boring routines of being a gull. With other "spiritually awakened" gulls, Jonathan finds a "higher plane of existence" where no heaven resides; where perfecting his knowledge becomes his mission; where he discovers satisfaction in his tenacity to learn; and where he gains a metaphysical wisdom that transports him across mystical dimensions.

As an enlightened seagull among boring, normal seabirds, Jonathan gathers other outlaws like himself who are true to themselves and embrace freedom. Among likeminded seekers of Truth, he finds peace . . .

I, too, gathered with "likeminded seekers" of ultimate knowledge. One of these seekers was Sheila, a troubled young woman whom I met at a party.

Liquor flowed like water there, and we struck up a friendship that became intimate over the next few months. As we played on beaches or studied together, I ignored the signs that Sheila had fallen in love with me.

One day I realized that our conversations were drifting into marriage territory, so I simply and clumsily broke off the relationship. It didn't go well...

I avoided Sheila at college, assuming that her broken heart had mended, until one night her friends told me about her accident. Sheila had consumed too much alcohol at a party and lost her balance on a high veranda. She had fallen to her death.

I knew Sheila quite well. I knew a little about her childhood, her family, and her dreams.

Did I share some responsibility for her death? Had she turned to excessive drinking to forget the pain of my rejection?

A profound sense of guilt consumed me, and I asked myself: *Where does this empathy come from? Does my conscience manufacture sorrow, or does something or "someone" outside of my being inspire remorse?*

And even more thought provoking: Where was Sheila now?

I refocused my mind upon studies, targeting a degree in Agricultural Commerce (farm management, valuation, and dairy science), but it took months for my haunting guilt to subside. After exhausting the hands-on fieldwork at local farms, my school required me to gain experience at sheep and cattle farms on the South Island and in New Zealand's Southern Alps.

Traveling to the farthest reaches of New Zealand—where cultures differed according to climate and heritage—whetted my appetite to explore beyond the borders of my island nation.

The opportunity came to cross the Tasman Sea and work in Australia, and I jumped at the chance.

KIWI IN THE OUTBACK

In the Land Down Under, I faced challenges that rivaled the untamed perils of the surf and sea.

Before I lived in Australia, I used the word "outback" interchangeably with our Kiwi expression "wop wops." But in Australia, I discovered the outback to be a desolate, deadly wilderness larger than Europe and twenty-nine times larger than my beautiful New Zealand.

To complete my required Lincoln University field studies, I landed a job in the outback with a family at Frankton, New South Wales. They owned an 8,000-acre cattle and sheep station (ranch). I had never known such merciless demands by employers before, nor had any labor I performed in New Zealand prepared me for my job as an Australian jackaroo (sheep herder/cowhand).

Mr. and Mrs. LeHay—whose wizened faces were sunburnt the same ochre color as Aussie dirt—tested their fair-haired surfer dude with barn duties and hand milking the "house cows" morning and night. I soon graduated to the most disgusting farm work that this Kiwi had undertaken to date: "Mulesing" sheep.

Mulesing entailed slicing off the fleshy flap of skin from around a Merino lamb's breech to prevent fly strikes (infestations). Hundreds of sheep in stock pens awaited my attention, and I retreated to my room at night exhausted and homesick as the days turned to weeks of feverish 110-degree heat.

Then the season abruptly changed. Rain deluged the station, accompanied by unbearable humidity. Scorpions skittered from their nests, and half-a-dozen of the LeHays' Kelpies and Blue Heelers (dogs) patrolled the corrals and yard for black mambas, brown snakes, and adders. It was common to kill hand-sized spiders before using the outdoor shower or long drop.

No matter how unappealing the task, I made it my mission to learn every aspect of running an Aussie station—though a few of the Aussie-born jackaroos, or experienced farm hands, expected the Kiwi surfer to run back home with his tail between his legs. Only by digging fence posts in the outdoor furnace and sloshing in warm muck to rescue lambs (without whining) did I win grudging respect.

The hard-bitten jackaroos let me know when I measured up. They welcomed me to "boil the billy" (make tea) for them and even share a cuppa. At campfires I smoked a rollie sometimes, too, while having a blow (a rest).

When the LeHays tasked me as a bore runner (checking remote water reservoirs), it suited me. I drove a motorcycle and carried a rifle to kill predators. In the outback, the moon shone across the landscape like a slow-moving lantern. Lying beneath the grandeur of stars, I sensed that someone sat at my campfire with me.

Was it God?

The chirring of nightjars and the occasional scream of a curlew distracted me from thoughts about Mum. If she was right, and God was real, I had failed him utterly. I drifted off to sleep, resolving once again to live life to the fullest with no regrets.

Aboriginal lore cast light upon my esoteric quest for fulfillment. Indigenous youth of Australia ventured upon an odyssey of self-discovery in the outback. A "walkabout" was an Aboriginal rite of passage that ultimately fused nomadic longings to every aspect of their lives—their occupations, relationships, and worldview.

Few Aussies (outside of the indigenous Aboriginal peoples) grasped the significance of this journey of self-awareness. But I understood it. My own walkabout had just begun.

MERMAID BEACH

I packed my kit, bound for my new and final Lincoln University field requirements. The prospect of working on a farm in a different region of Australia excited me. A bus delivered me to a well-known station, where, from horizon to horizon, cattle grazed 10,000 acres of pasturelands alongside another 10,000 acres of wheat fields.

As a jackaroo, I was worth my salt. I had proven myself at Frankton, drinking my share of Toohey's beer with my mates. I had crowded into a truck bed with other jackaroos and caroused at the only pub within a hundred miles—then worked the next day with a clanging hangover.

I had killed my share of snakes and boars that threatened the LeHays' sheep and had eaten dust from mobs of cattle. I thrived as an Aussie stockman. And best of all, I had absorbed a wealth of livestock knowledge impossible to attain in a classroom.

I admired the LeHays for their harsh but fair treatment of their workers, but after months of apprenticeship, I was glad to leave them in the dust.

At Kansas Station, anticipation crowded out all my previous history. My heart leapt at possibilities. Rows of Massey Ferguson threshing machines and International Harvester tractors huddled like a rugby team set for the opening whistle!

My new boss, a Kansan from America, took a liking to me right away. He looked me up and down, and I passed muster, especially since I had a heavy truck license.

The station manager turned me loose with all manner of cropping equipment, and occasionally warned: "Keep them rows straight, lad!" and "Tighten up them turns!"

Threshing grain reawakened the plowman inside me as we harvested wheat in the glare of tractor headlights. At the end of harvest season, the Kansan paid me well.

He recognized my love of soil and livestock, and as an inducement to remain in Australia; he tempted me with 100 acres of prime agricultural land. (More than one jackaroo had ended up a millionaire in the Land Down Under).

But my mandatory field studies had ended. I visited the main office to tell the generous Kansan, "Yeah, nah. But thanks, mate." I packed up my kit, proud that I finished what I had started.

With my wad of cash, and just a few months away from graduating with a degree, I bought an EK Holden and headed for Queensland for a vacation before leaving Oz.

If lust had a voice, it would have shrieked like a kookaburra at Mermaid Beach in Queensland. "Virtue" barely registered on my scale of morality—but revelry couldn't drown out two reproachful voices of decency: Mum wrote to update me on family and reminded me that she was praying for me. And I corresponded with a young woman named Kerry.

I had met Kerry at a music festival at Hamilton months before I left New Zealand. Kerry had been writing letters to me faithfully while I worked in Australia, and I answered when I found time. We shared a long-distance relationship due to our mutual acquaintances in New Zealand. For me, it was nothing more than friendship.

I set up my partying base at the Mermaid Beach Surf Club in Queensland and caroused late and often. I purchased a prime surfboard for catching the breaks at Burleigh Head (a cape piercing into the Coral Sea). I also surfed Kirra at the City of Gold Coast and rode wave barrels at Stradie/Stradbroke Island like few I had ever known.

I should have been satisfied. I should have felt fulfilled. I surfed the most beautiful waves on earth and spent days with amazing friends—each, like me, longing for a trustworthy, sustaining sense of belonging.

But at night, when I was alone in my bungalow, I drank to deaden my conscience. I was blind, leading others who were blind, while the sands of time poured through an hourglass held in God's gentle, sovereign hands.

ABYSS OF LONGING

When I returned to New Zealand from the Land Down Under, my life felt as if I had veered off course. My future was uncharted and my destiny depressing. Gone were kangaroos to dodge on motorbikes or crocs to kill on my rounds in the Australian outback. Gone were rowdy stockmen with whom I bandied friendly curses and drank beer.

My motivation idled with three flat tires. I longed to find a job that fit my adventurous lifestyle. To fill a gnawing emptiness, I dived or surfed unexplored reefs up and down the New Zealand coast.

I finished up my degree in Agricultural Commerce, receiving an A in my major of Dairy Science. Every week I sifted through job offers—rejecting any that might chain me to a desk.

Mum and Dad had attended my graduation ceremony at Lincoln. My siblings dutifully filled niches in society. My brother Neil served in the New Zealand Army and my sister Sharon worked in nursing.

I abandoned Lincoln forever and headed for the North Island. There, I stayed with *rellies* (Kiwi for relatives) until moving to Rotorua with my Celtic childhood mate, Jack. My old friend had flunked out of law school but found a consuming pleasure in a hobby-turned-obsession: horticulture.

We made a great team. I supplied the rent money, and Jack contributed his knowhow growing marijuana in areas outside of town. I admired his diligent research in cultivating some of the most potent plants on the North Island.

When I stayed at our family bach at Waihi Beach, I tiptoed respectfully around my grandmother's old-fashioned morality. She watched me from her living room like a harrier hawk and judged most of my friends to be "trashy."

Except Cynthia.

Cynthia worked for a modeling agency, and I was happy to discover that the woman of my dreams lived in Auckland, only a couple hours from our beach home. Even my grandmother approved of Cynthia, and I fell head-over-heels in love.

Tanned, fit, and restless, I was sick of being alone. I invited this wonderful woman to spend Easter holidays with my family—scheming to secure "alone time" away from my vigilant grandmother whose duty (it seemed) was to guard my virtue.

On Easter weekend, Cynthia was late in arriving. I glanced at clocks several times, wondering if she had forgotten about coming. The phone finally rang, and a mutual friend delivered devastating news from Auckland.

"Last night Cynthia was in a car accident, Ian. I'm sorry. She's... *gone.* She's dead, bro."

For a few seconds, I felt too numb to grasp the reality of the report. Then it hit me. *It's happening again! A woman I care for has died. Am I destined for tragedy in my relationships?*

I fled to the sea for days, where waves of guilt overwhelmed me.

Did my impure motives on Easter weekend play a part in Cynthia's death?

And I wondered: *Where is she now?*

Jack commiserated with me in his own way—by offering me doobies from his special stash. Weed blunted the edges of my remorse, but I needed something more potent. I needed help in answering existential questions that Cynthia's death churned up.

I delved into books about psychedelic "trips" and learned about magic mushrooms, mescaline, and peyote by first-hand experience. I hoped to open portals to ethereal realms if they existed, and I yearned to find the missing link to complete my personal destiny.

I inhabited two contrasting realms: one where I lived as a typical Kiwi holding a position on the New Zealand Dairy Board; the other where I engaged in yoga and forms of Asian meditation, using hallucinogens to contact whomever or whatever forces might possess the keys to ultimate knowledge.

My chosen vocation of dairy management fascinated me. I loved the science of soils and traveled to hundreds of farms, consulting with dairymen and women who required counsel on pasture management, milk yield, or budget.

I would have been shocked had I known my future. Troubleshooting for the Dairy Board prepared me for a labor of love that I judged to be totally irrational at the time.

CHEECH AND CHONG

Pointless.

Jack's incentive to become an attorney drifted in a cannabis fog, and I joined him in my own vaporous adventure. Cultivating and supplying other "dope heads" filled our safe with cash but offered us no sense of purpose.

What should we do next?

"Maybe it's time for me to buy a dairy. Or raise sheep."

Jack laughed and handed me a lit joint.

"It's all pointless, Ian."

I turned the television volume up where our counterculture heroes, Cheech and Chong, stumbled across the screen. They performed a dope-addled comedy routine, and I snickered at their antics, realizing that weed failed to numb my brain as efficiently as it once did. In fact, with every toke, I sucked in gloom . . . Jack was right. My career success felt pointless.

I tried to focus.

Should I change vocations? If only I could clear away the clouds obscuring my destiny once and for all.

Members of *The Beatles* musical group had traveled to Northern India. Upon their return to England, they touted Transcendental Meditation as a spiritual breakthrough in their lives. *Should I seek out the ashram of Maharishi Mahesh Yogi like they did? Is what I searched for hiding in some remote Asian culture?*

I, too, craved an epiphany. I needed a revelation to jar me out of practical, rational behavior—and my oracle came! It popped up like a submerged buoy while Jack and I watched a movie called *Endless Summer*.

In virtual rapture, we "accompanied" surfing icons on their incredible "everlasting summer around the world." My heart nearly beat out of my chest! I imagined myself challenging surf in Senegal, Ghana, Nigeria, South Africa, Australia, Tahiti, California, and Hawaii—like they did.

Endless Summer on the big screen also dazzled me with scenes of New Zealand. A longing for true freedom seized me—an unrestrained license to experience life wherever and however I chose. The most talented surfers in the world declared a compelling message to my disillusioned generation and to me—stop conforming. Throw off the shackles of expectation and live life to the fullest! Just go for it!

But what about my job with the Dairy Board?

I was 24 years old when I defied my father and ignored my mum's tears to embark on my personal "OE." An OE (overseas experience) is known to New Zealanders as a Kiwi's rite of passage, much like an Aussie's walkabout.

Jack and I spent days mapping out a hypothetical circuit of pleasure, and the plan became reality when I quit my job with the dairy board. Few in my family understood my decision—a "riptide" of adventure took hold of me.

I persuaded my parents to drop Jack and me at the Auckland Airport, where Kerry (my correspondent and friend) hugged me. My parents and Kerry were three people who represented morality and restraint in my life— and I couldn't wait to leave them behind. Once again, I promised Kerry that I wouldn't forget to write.

"When will you be back, Ian?" Kerry asked, aware that I had set no date for a return flight home.

"I don't know when," I said.

I had said the same thing to my disappointed employers at the Dairy Board.

Stepping onto the blazing Qantas tarmac in Sydney, I was confident that fate favored me. My mental and physical abilities had often overruled karma—whether challenged by the treachery of man, beast, or nature. Our trip appeared to be "ordained by the gods."

In Australia, Jack and I hitched a ride to Queensland where I reestablished old surfing acquaintances at Mermaid Beach. Jack and I had sold our latest marijuana crop grown in Rotorua, and I had deposited my last Dairy Board paychecks into my personal account.

We were chuffed (Kiwi for excited) about getting to undiscovered, exotic surf breaks and Asian cities, where we could legally buy "enlightening" hallucinogens and psychedelic drugs. Along our OE itinerary, I had anticipated surfing the perfect wave—still aching to reach a new level of consciousness and find a reason for living.

Bewitched by visions of "paradise," I failed to glance behind me at the shadow dogging my steps.

CRAZY KIWI

We couldn't wait to "escape" from Australia…

After weeks of surfing the East Coast of Australia, we ended up at Surfers Paradise (the resort on Queensland's Gold Coast). We hitchhiked or hopped on buses to the hottest breaks, like Bryon Bay and Lennox Head along the coast. Aussies weren't necessarily welcoming to Kiwis at some beaches, and we set our sights beyond their breaks.

In a fit of thrift, I came up with a brilliant idea. "Let's take a shortcut through the outback, Jack. We can fly out of Darwin to Bali and work our way through Indonesia. It'll save us heaps…"

Jack imagined the outback of Australia to be a drier version of the wop wops of New Zealand, so he heartily agreed with "Sweet as!"

He was getting impatient to sample the herbal delights he heard were readily available in Asia.

With backpack and surfboards, we two scruffy Kiwis set off across Queensland and the barren Northern Territory—rescued periodically by pubs and wary barkeeps on our route to Darwin. I loved sleeping beneath the stars again, remembering how to comb every inch of my sleeping bag for spiders and scorpions.

Amused cattle jackaroos hauled us two "daft Kiwi surfers" as far as Mount Isa, a mining town halfway to our destination. We opted to pay for a bus ride on the last thousand miles to Darwin, a city that held no attraction for us. It was the season when sea wasps migrated into the reefs. Since surfing wasn't a viable option after being warned about the "killer jellies," we bought our airfare to Bali.

In Bali, I believed that I had finally *arrived*.

At a beachfront bungalow (called a losmen) at Kuta Reef, I lay alone on my cot. Jack had snuck away for his own decadent adventure, and I rested weary limbs after battling left-hand breaks for several hours. Drifting in and out of a hashish haze, I wondered why the same pointless mood possessed me here in "paradise" that troubled me back home in New Zealand.

Am I not living the dream?

Thousands of Europeans flocked to Bali's hedonistic playgrounds to experience the legendary hospitality. Merchants in shops and on street corners hawked colorful textiles and jewelry and knew where to acquire a variety of mind-expanding drugs for experimenting in an exquisite beachfront environment.

Europeans who were curious and brave enough to dive deeply into Hindu society observed unnatural marvels rooted in ancient mysticism. Balinese graven images of Buddha, elephants, birds, and mythological creatures represented benign and vile entities.

Before construction of hotels, shamans were consulted to placate spirits prior to erecting pillars or deciding where to place doorways.

A shaman laid down invisible "energy lines" as boundaries where engineers paid homage to spirits if encountering equipment failures.

Images with open mouths, sharp teeth, and elongated, lolling tongues decorated the entrances of Balinese homes and businesses. Families built shrines and appeased demons by offering them rice and fruit every day. Shamans were believed to transfigure into headless creatures or snakes and monkeys to exact devotion.

Discovery of the Balinese permissiveness and tolerance had given rise to a flood of European pleasure seekers. The islanders furnished everything that Europeans desired—resorts, fishing, surfing, drugs, mementos, and exotic food—against a backdrop of pristine beaches and mountains. When I visited homes, hotels, or temples, the wonderful people of Bali exuded a wary vigilance. They believed that spiritual entities were listening to every word they spoke and must be consulted about decisions.

In Bali, a single thread of virtue held me from drowning in self-indulgence—and the strand felt near to severing. If a hidden source of peace and harmony existed in Indonesia, I was desperate to find it.

ULUWATU

I couldn't leave Bali before surfing the spectacular left-hand reef breaks at Uluwatu.

A long, treacherous trail snaked down to the Uluwatu beach where a massive cave gorged upon the turquoise sea then spat it out again. Nearby, surfers traveled the outbound tide to line up, then rode inside incredible roiling barrels.

Adrenaline surged in me as an experienced local surfer's warning echoed against the jagged cave walls: "If you lose your board into a sea cave, leave it! Swim to shore. People die here!"

We left the cave entrance, and I set my sights on the beautiful waves in the distance. I utilized the rip to bring me into the lineup. I was well away from the saber-toothed cave when I mounted my board for a long, beautiful ride.

Uluwatu, Bali temple

But Uluwatu had other plans. My fifth wave closed out on me.

I tumbled under tons of saltwater, and my leash plug popped free of my surfboard! Untethered from the leg rope, my board bobbed, higgledy-piggledy, en route to the coral cave's saw-toothed gullet.

I followed the board with my eyes for a few seconds, calculating its replacement value. Then I made my decision. I swam after it, aiming my nose like a seal and pounding out fierce strokes.

But just as I laid hold of my prize, I felt cold fingers dragging my board and me toward the whitewater at the coral cavern. It seemed an eternity, but the deadly current loosened its grip—just for an instant—and I battled free. I bellied onto my board and paddled to shore, where my animated Balinese guide cursed at me in broken English.

He didn't understand. To a hardcore surfer, their surfboard was very precious, especially when traveling in a remote region where the cost to replace the board was unaffordable for the average surfer.

SHARKS AND DEMONS

As Jack and I traveled north through Jakarta and into Singapore and Malaysia, our destinies were beginning to diverge upon separate roads. We shared a fascination with remote mountain temples where priests (often sated with hashish) invited us to partake in their rituals. I usually relished these Asian adventures, but in Malaysia, as we sampled drugs and their foreign culture, their practices began to grate upon my soul.

The worship of idols resurrected a childhood memory that prickled a nerve. I remembered one of God's Ten Commandments ("Thou shalt have no other gods before thee or bow down to a graven image or idol").

In South East Asia, priests bathed their gods in costly oils, and poverty-stricken villagers sacrificed their family's rice to wooden idols. Hindus, Muslims, and Buddhists seemed to all be driven by fear! I had immersed myself in their lifestyles, devouring every pleasure that my senses could consume, yet I still felt as hollow as an empty petrol drum.

But Jack's yearning for the occult seemed insatiable. He tried to convince me that India held the answers to our existential questions.

I just wanted to surf.

The most exquisite waves in the world break along the coastlines of Malaysia. Months had passed on my grand OE, and Kerry's letters were making me a bit homesick as well.

Not Jack.

He gazed longingly toward cities like Calcutta and Madras, where he believed his search was leading him. We agreed to explore Malaysia together before he left for India. I staked out our route to dive at Tioman Island, 32 miles from the Malaysian mainland. From Mersing, on Peninsular Malaysia's east coast, we hitched a ride aboard a local fishing boat and landed at Tioman Island in the South China Sea—known the world over as a prime diving and surfing destination.

Backpacking to an unspoiled cove on Tioman Island, I rifled through my pack for snorkeling gear. The cove I had chosen for a day-trip teemed with aquatic life. I hoped to encounter sea turtles along a reef where the sun glinted off coral beneath water as clear as glass.

Less than an hour into my dive I noticed that I had ventured far beyond what I had originally planned. I floated on my back, absorbing the sunrays for a few moments before heading back to the beach—when a splash startled me.

Sharks…

Through my facemask, I counted three black-tipped reef sharks lazily sizing me up. Round and round, they circled in a practiced death ritual. I could have reached out and touched their gleaming, gray hides as they passed. Divers know that when sharks swim from their circle, they often attack in a frenzy.

I decided to break up their caper before they chose to "feed."

Like a torpedo, I swam for a protruding rock near shore. One shark swam behind me, inches from my toes. When it dropped back, another, approximately twice my size, swam alongside me like an escort.

I knew not to show fear as that is known to incite a shark's attack. Trembling, I rolled my frame atop sharp barnacles. Then, standing on the rock like Neptune, I belted out, "Hey! I almost died today!"

My declaration echoed ashore, and a group of divers waved. The sharks' dorsal fins slid beneath the waves and disappeared, leaving me to ponder what it might have meant to be food for fishes.

Another close call in life's journey!

In Malaysia, another disturbing brush with death came as Jack and I explored Taman Negara, the oldest rainforest in the world. We believed that our new friend, Mr. Lee, was acquainted with the mountain trails to waterfalls and stunning viewpoints through the dense jungle.

We were wrong.

We were unarmed, but the park rangers assured us that the Malayan tigers usually hunted at night and most often fled when encountering humans. Of course, tigers were exactly what Jack and I hoped to see as we donned backpacks for our jungle daytrip. We were also hoping to see orangutans, elephants, and even rhinoceroses that lived in the area.

We confidently set out upon a trail. Soon, we outpaced Mr. Lee, leaving him to catch up. He seemed winded, but amid the otherworldly flora and fauna that surrounded us, we were glad to take our scenic route closer to his pace. Our memorable time spent in the rainforest would never be forgotten…

We ended our excursion that evening as we hiked into the ranger headquarters where we had started. We flumped our packs off, and Jack asked offhandedly, "Where's Mr. Lee, Ian?"

I glanced down the trail. "He was right behind us, wasn't he?"

It struck Jack and me at the same instant. We hadn't seen him for an hour or more! After our last viewpoint, we had bounded ahead of Mr. Lee at a blistering pace.

It was nearly dusk when we alerted the Taman Negara Park rangers—and they couldn't have cared less that our Chinese friend was missing.

"We go find him tomorrow," a captain in sweat-stained fatigues informed us. His lackadaisical attitude lit my fuse, and I demanded that he send a search party. He refused.

At the park entrance, I consulted with Jack and two Austrian lads who had just arrived after their trek. We decided to backtrack and find Mr. Lee ourselves. We refilled canteens and hoped to locate our friend before the Malayan park rangers came out to search for him too.

The lights from the Taman Negara ranger station faded in the distance. Night screams, insects, and birdcalls brewed with our shouts for Mr. Lee.

We backtracked along our daylight route until our torches grew dim, and within two hours we found our friend. He was terrified, bruised, and shivering. He seemed to have lost all memory of the Queen's English and jabbered in a dialect none of us knew. It wasn't difficult to interpret his grateful tears.

A palpable darkness blanketed the five of us as we strained to find the trail leading back to the ranger station. When our last torch flickered out, every path disappeared completely.

Now *we* needed to be rescued!

Jungle heat gave way to a bone-chilling cold. The chill penetrated Mr. Lee's frame, and I knew he wouldn't last the night without heat. In fact, all five of us were underdressed for a hypothermic night in Taman Negara. Cozying up against one another, with Mr. Lee in the center, we huddled like a wobbly, spent rugby team, awaiting daylight.

We might have slept a little had we been able to ignore the scavengers and stalkers peering at us through the undergrowth, snapping branches, or slithering nearby. We dug out rocks to hurl at any creatures that sounded close enough to choke or rend us. A sliver of moon sometimes gave away a yellow-eyed beast's location.

At daybreak, bird trills replaced echoes of menacing night fauna, and landmarks pointed us to the ranger station. Our bedraggled crew arrived just in time to meet indigenous Orang Asli trackers. They had been employed by the rangers and were setting out to find us, blowguns in hand.

It wasn't long after our sojourn in the Taman Negara that Jack and I prepared to part ways. Before he left, we peeled one more layer from the gentle façade of religious fervor that the people of Malaysia demonstrated.

Whether Hindu, Buddhist, or Muslim, I sensed within their devotion sentient beings that influenced and manipulated our hosts.

Jack and I visited Penang Island, where Jack persuaded me to accompany him to, what he believed to be, a tried-and-true way to breach the spiritual barrier between our reality and the unseen world around us. Two Chinese "guides" promised to care for us during the experience, and rather than lead us to a dingy Malaysian opium den, they carted us off to a Buddhist temple.

"Why are we here?" I asked them.

Jack didn't seem bothered by their answer, but I grew uneasy about our ethereal "tour" when they told us, "We must appease the opium god before we go."

Inside the temple, a statue of Buddha stared at us, bare-bellied with a wide grin. To his left sat a lesser, subservient "god." To Buddha's right was a statue they called the opium god. Worshipers had piled dark, raw opium at least two feet deep. Reverently, our two guides deposited some of *their* opium before we ceremonially backed out of the room.

I followed our wizened Chinese mentors back to their tuk-tuk, my nerves thoroughly unstrung. Pangs of guilt assaulted me, but I wasn't about to allow a childish attack of conscience to steal my opportunity to experience an unnatural adventure. After all, wasn't this one of the reasons I was in Asia?

Our tour guides didn't knock as we followed them into the opium den. I could feel a collective consciousness emanating from the graven images around me, but I believed that my personal moxie would buffer or barricade me against harm, as it always had.

Our guides escorted us to beds and lit our opium pipes. I felt a strange, silky sensation overwhelm my body. Hours later, we slowly recovered our senses. In hindsight, at this stage of my OE, I was naively answering an invitation to consort with demonic spirits. Unwittingly, I had crossed a line, and there was no going back.

Jack and I parted amicably in Singapore. He flew to India, seeking deeper spiritual revelations, while I visited Sri Lanka to fill my surfing and diving bucket list. I had to iron out visa problems too.

Friends in New Zealand helped me connect with a Tamil Hindu family living in Colombo, the capitol of Sri Lanka, and they welcomed me with open arms. I felt no caution as I stayed at their home and accompanied them to festivals and temples to worship. They treated me like part of their family.

The fascinating Tamil culture had survived multiple dynasties, preserved through music and strong Hindu animistic beliefs. Every morning the family offered fruit and flowers to Ganesh, a brightly painted stone elephant idol. Ganesh was the god who championed intellectuals and businessmen, as well as being the patron of scribes and authors.

My Tamil friends' rituals varied from day to day. Sometimes they bathed Ganesh in water or milk. Other days they dressed the elephant in beautiful scarves and clothing. I was mildly interested in their reverence for the image, until one day I felt a "presence" seep through its eyes and *touch* me. I recoiled, remembering the entity that tried to inhabit me when my Grandfather Arthur died.

Do my Hindu friends possess a piece of the existential puzzle that I yearn to find? I wondered.

A valuable year had slipped through my hands, and I had yet to find a drug, an adventure, or a sensual encounter to satisfy my hunger for true peace. In Asia, I had cast a net wider than ever before to discover what lay beyond earthly visible life. In Sri Lanka, I was on the brink of knowing more, and it seemed that mystical beings welcomed me.

As a proud freethinker, I felt no need to hang any "no trespassing" sign on the gates of mind, body, or spirit. So, I felt privileged when my Tamil friends escorted me to the Hidden City to see the Kataragama temple. The temple complex had been dedicated to the guardian deity of Sri Lanka, Kataragama, and the Hindu war god, Murugan.

After an arduous climb on jungle trails, we entered through the compound's gate and toured shrines venerated by several pagan faiths. I observed these worshipers, fascinated by their zeal for inanimate figures—until an image of Kataragama diverted my attention. Kataragama's lips were *moving*. The idol spoke to me in some tongue foreign to me!

I informed one of my guides about the freakish event.

He shrugged. "It's not unusual," he said with a smile.

Feeling very uneasy, I made my way past glassy-eyed, ash-smeared priests on my way to the exit. I ambled past gaudy shrines and found the entrance where screams from the rooftop startled me. I stopped dead. Red-faced monkeys, their teeth bared, swung from ornamental parapets and shrieked at me. None pounced, but they continued to screech with clenched fists until I left the compound. I felt as though the monkeys knew I sensed something was wrong and were not at all happy with me. Later, I was to discover that many Hindus worship the monkey god Hanuman.

I waited outside for my friends to come out of the Kataragama temple.

To seal my memories of Sri Lanka, I traveled to Kandy to witness the Kandy Perahera Temple festival. Lines of fire dancers and frenzied performers waved palm fronds in concert with Asian elephants outfitted with multicolored masks. The pachyderms were draped in giant purple and orange capes, and their ears fanned in unison with great methodical strides.

Dignified attendants holding spears escorted the gentle beasts. The elephants' tusks had been dipped in liquid gold especially for the Kandy Perahera celebration.

Thousands of Sri Lankans celebrated the good fortune and national protection obtained from worshiping the centuries-old Buddha's tooth. It was said to have been salvaged from Buddha's cremated remains and would keep growing forever. At the festival of Perahera, the supernatural tooth was displayed for Buddhists and Hindus to revere.

CHAPTER 3

GALAXY

Escape from Arugam

After renewing my passport, I left my Tamil friends at Colombo and arrived at Arugam Bay. It was there that I met Mark, an Australian sailor, and we struck up a friendship with drugs as a mutual interest. Mark tried my hashish and nodded appreciatively.

• 49

He handed me several rupees and pocketed the kilo-size baggie I offered. We continued our stroll along the Arugam Bay pier. Yachts and boats of every shape and condition docked on either side of the wharf. Some gleamed bright, trim, and tidy, bobbing in the evening sun. Others listed like drunken sailors, their oil-streaked hulls peppered with barnacles.

Mark and I drifted into a pub and stepped up to the bar for a beer to seal the deal.

I had been sampling beaches and surfing the enormous waves on the east coast of Sri Lanka for a month or more. I mentioned to Mark that I was ready to move on and needed transportation to Jeffreys Bay, South Africa—to polish off my OE surfing tour.

"We're sailing that way," Mark said casually. "You interested in joining a crew for a few weeks? I'm a bosun's mate on a yacht. We could use a hard-working Kiwi aboard the *Galaxy*. You game?"

By the end of our conversation, Mark had audited my limitations as a sailor and happily discovered that I was an experienced diver—a valuable crewmember to have on a voyage.

"Why not? I'd love to go."

"Good. I'll introduce you to the owner of the schooner. We're finishing up repairs. We have some mending to do below the water line. She leaks a tad..."

Leaks? I should have asked more questions before committing, but I approached my new challenge like I did every other venture. I believed in my own resourcefulness—it had always saved me.

Mark hadn't lied to me exactly—*Galaxy* was a wooden schooner with a storied past. It was true that the double-mast yacht had tied up at many third-world ports of call. Built in the '40s, *Galaxy* had sailed on the Southern California racing circuit and survived many storms.

What Mark kept to himself was the fact that *Galaxy* had recently been towed off a jagged reef. A gouge in its keel had been patched before resuming the circumnavigation dream of *Galaxy's* owner.

Mark introduced me to *Galaxy's* skipper, a thin, over-tanned woman who welcomed me with a raised coconut shell full of gin.

Captain Audrey reflected the overall condition of her worn, weathered schooner, and she called Dean, the *Galaxy's* navigator, to meet me. Dean stuck his hash pipe between his teeth and extended a hand. He was Audrey's son.

"Show 'im the boat," Audrey ordered, and Mark nodded deferentially. Out of earshot, he assured me that the six-member crew (including me) was more than sufficient to sail a two-master. *Galaxy* just needed a few more days in port to "get 'er ship shape."

I stowed my duffle bag (and doubts) below deck and tested an empty bunk next to *Galaxy's* cook, a Mauritian islander named Berto who spoke English, French, and Creole. Berto mentored me in boat protocol.

Another adventure . . . this time aboard a 96-foot schooner. Perfect! I speculated.

My first job as the newest member of the crew was scraping barnacles from *Galaxy's* hull. A million arthropods clung to the yacht. While scraping off these barnacles, I discovered the "patch" in *Galaxy's* keel. A reef had gouged a hole, and a brass "Band-Aid" had been screwed and glued over it.

Tears in the sails had been stitched up, and by my rookie reckoning, our boat appeared seaworthy at last. Most of the *Galaxy's* final repairs had been completed when Audrey roused us from our bunks well before dawn.

"Up! We're getting underway! Let's go!"

Topside, I glanced at the dark skyline against which silhouettes of fishing boats worked the morning tide. Mark motioned me to help him shove *Galaxy* away from the wharf. A puff of wind filled our sails, sending us silently toward fishermen at the mouth of the bay. Nothing on the dock behind us stirred.

"This is pretty dangerous, isn't it?" I asked Mark, who shrugged resignedly.

We were running without lights, and suddenly lanterns on a fleet of fishing boats lit up the calm sea ahead. Sri Lankan curses from shirtless fishermen wafted louder and louder as we approached.

I glanced at the helm where Audrey and Dean stood, and Cap Audrey commanded the course Dean was to follow. He spun the helm to correct—and plowed across the top of a fishing net. *Galaxy* jerked to a stop. Everyone stared at the only diver on the boat...

Audrey was yelling at me. "Don't just stand there! Get down there and cut us loose!"

Dean handed me a rigging knife, and I grabbed a snorkel mask and torch and let myself down into the cool sea. I had a good idea where the fishing net was hung up. I followed the lead line to where it had wedged on an edge of the brass plate at the base of the keel.

Why should I cut the net and ruin a day's fishing for the fishermen? I thought.

Instead, I hauled on the lead line with all my strength while the fishing boat, several feet away, fed me an inch or two of slack. I quickly yanked the net free as our two-master lurched out of its predicament.

The lead line, as taut as a bowstring, snapped close to my legs and nearly caught me as it lunged away into the darkness of the sea. Mission accomplished. I resurfaced at the stern of the yacht with my lungs ready to burst. I made it to the surface seconds before *Galaxy* swayed under a slow, powerful gale. Amid the fishermen's shouts of relief, I climbed aboard, and we sailed into the murky dawn.

I wasn't fishing for compliments, and none came from Cap Audrey or Dean. Daylight overtook *Galaxy*, and I held my peace about the whole precarious affair until the evening. I asked Berto why we had bolted from the Sri Lanka port without running lights or engine.

He chuckled. "Our boat has been in Trincomalee Harbor for three months. Cap Audrey decided that she couldn't or wouldn't pay the mooring and duty fees for *Galaxy*. We're running for international waters. The Maritime Coast Guard can't touch us there!"

Officials never overtook *Galaxy* before we entered "safe" waters out of Sri Lankan jurisdiction. I breathed a sigh of relief, recalling the horror stories about expatriates jailed in Asian prisons, never to be heard from again. For three days, we sailed without changing course. But any sailor worth his salt knows that the Indian Ocean is never "safe..."

TWIN FUNNELS

Early in the morning, three days into our voyage, Cap Audrey screamed for us to awaken. We scrambled to the deck for orders. Mark had spotted a waterspout, and we seemed to be on a collision course. Above the funnel, fretful clouds spread across the horizon igniting bolts of lightning at frightening intervals.

"Blimey! See that, Dean? Another one!" Mark hollered to our awestruck navigator. He pointed, but all eyes were already glued to the skyline. The storm had birthed a twin waterspout, sinuously dancing and sucking the ocean up into it like a tornado. The ocean responded to the erratic high-pressure colliding with low pressure by plowing up the waves and piling them against the *Galaxy*.

If one spout hits us, it will do a lot of damage! We're done, I thought as a pinpoint of fear bored into my soul.

The twin waterspouts undulated within 30 yards of us before whirling erratically past the *Galaxy* like two volatile thoroughbreds—the first spurred to the port side, the other paralleled the starboard. It seemed that the worst was over, and my relief latched onto the utter impossibility of what I had seen.

"Batten Down! Close all the hatches! Secure the deck!"

Audrey stood beside Dean at the helm, sober as a judge. She screamed into Dean's ear to steer for a seam of crystalline blue sky far ahead, but the wind clasped *Galaxy* like a giant's hand, holding her in place. We bobbed like a toy in a tub until a massive shadow engulfed us. An unpredictable gale whipped us sideways, and then tipped us heavenward before tossing us into cavernous troughs again and again. I tripped and slid on the deck, holding onto anything nailed or screwed down.

With sails still unfurled, Dean steered along an endless curtain of dark clouds draped along the horizon, hoping to outrun the blow. I descended below deck, shocked to find seawater sloshing about my ankles.

"We're taking on water!" I hollered toward the wheelhouse, knowing exactly where the seepage into our sinking vessel originated. The patch on the keel had loosened.

Audrey seemed to awaken from her frozen state. She yelled, "Turn on the bilge pump, you idiot!"

Mark tried to crank the old pump, but the schooner's main batteries were dead. So were the backup cells. Audrey had drained the storage cells with hours of constant cooling of her gin and coconut arrack—none of the battery cells had been recharged with the generator.

Sheets of rain showered *Galaxy* as our captain squawked (what I believed were senseless) orders to her crew. "Bring up the generator and secure it on the deck! Charge up the batteries."

"Is she daft?"

I was incredulous. Mark shook his head and slogged below. I glanced at Dean, glued to the helm, willing the slow-moving *Galaxy* toward a sunny slit in the clouds.

I tried to reason with our captain. "Cap! The gen will never kick over in these wet conditions. Leave it below, and we'll charge the batteries from there!"

The deck was awash in seawater, and waves kept breaking over the bow.

"No—we can't risk a fire! Bring it up to the deck."

We attached a hand winch to the generator, and two men hauled it topside, where foamy waves immediately doused it. Mark yanked the starter rope time and time again with no luck. Finally, Audrey ordered it taken below deck again amid curses and orders to "Fix it!"

After ferreting around in a box of corroded parts, I carried news topside that *Galaxy's* generator was "unfixable." We had no spare sparkplugs to replace the damaged ones.

No engine. No navigational lights. No power to run the bilge pump…
We're sinking in the Indian Ocean. Is this how my adventure ends? I asked myself.

We were elated to find an old hand-operated bilge pump below deck. Taking turns, the crew barely kept pace with the seawater leaking into *Galaxy's* belly. I glanced at the sails billowing wildly and helped Mark inspect the rigging.

Mark, aghast, pointed at the topping-lift cable that held up the 1,000-pound boom. The taut cable appeared frayed, as if rats had chewed it. He pointed out the hazard to Audrey, and I expected Dean or Audrey to order a repair. Instead, Audrey's panicky voice rose above the wind. "Drop the main sail!"

Mark and I froze. Mark complicated our predicament by cursing, then he crowded close to Audrey. Everyone on the deck stared at the pair as he lowered his voice like a pause in a gale.

"No, Cap."

He began explaining like he was reasoning with a child. "The sail is taking weight off the boom. If we drop the main, the boom will swing free and kill someone! And we may lose the boom altogether."

"I SAID take in the main sail!" Audrey spoke through gritted teeth—and two sailors obeyed her order.

The frayed topping-lift cable snapped, and the boom swung like an unwieldy tree trunk scattering Audrey's panicked crew. At the helm, Dean tacked the schooner into a wave to prevent the boom from crashing onto the crewmembers. And somehow as I yarded frantically on the sheet it fell into one of the three slots of the gallow beneath it and Mark and I lashed it into place.

The belligerent storm held us in its grip for 13 days. In lulls, we hand-stitched tears in the sails, replaced cables, and re-screwed and re-lashed whatever had jerked free from the deck. The Band-Aid repair on our keel required attention, but we couldn't do anything until we came to a safe port. We were able to hoist the main sail again after I repaired the frayed cable on the topping-lift.

From time immemorial a sailor's mettle has been tested during capricious, long-lasting cyclonic events like this one. The stress of balancing on a pitching, rolling deck, the terror of drowning, and the tension among crewmembers can bring a sailor to the breaking point.

Our refrigerated food had spoiled due to the negligence of our captain not keeping the batteries charged. Rice became our meal of the day, boiled by our harried, versatile cook, Berto.

Audrey stood at Dean's side as they decided to tack toward Mauritius, an island off the coast of South Africa. Dean managed stress by sucking fumes in his hash pipe. Audrey handled her stress with gin. They took turns at the wheel, often relieved by Mark or me in the night watches. No matter who manned the wheel, we sailed blind, squinting to see through volleys of rain and seawater.

Audrey seldom uttered a gracious word to any of us, and my opinion of her was compounded by a sobering moment on deck one day. The storm had taken a toll on my psyche, but my head cleared abruptly when I noticed a shadow "standing" behind Audrey. This was on a steel-gray day void of sunshine, and I stared in disbelief. The dark presence shifted independently from our captain's movements for several seconds before disappearing.

Of our six crewmembers, one sailor named Terrance spent much of the voyage seasick and curled on his bunk, nearly useless as a seaman. During the storm, he had come to the end of his mental endurance and cracked. In fact, the specter of drowning tormented all of us, and no one knew which of us might be next to fall apart.

One evening, after taking turns manning the bilge pump and eating a ration of rice, four of us sat together on deck, voicing our fears. We believed that *Galaxy* was doomed and groped for a morsel of solace from camaraderie—before dying.

I felt much the same as I had when huddling around hypothermic Mr. Lee in the Malaysian jungle. In Malaysia, we felt hemmed in by night predators. Here in the Indian Ocean, we battled fatigue and teetered at the edge of derangement—for *days*.

My beloved sea had betrayed me. Topside, I never knew when crushing waves would dash me to the schooner's deck. *Galaxy* floundered on a southwesterly course near the equator, and I felt as crippled inside as our battered schooner.

The cyclone had fractured an internal bulkhead of skepticism that I fiercely guarded. I had imbibed on Asian cultures, paganism, and carnal living for nearly two years and still wandered aimlessly without purpose.

Mauritius diving photos

Among the spiritless crew, in a moment of uncharacteristic humility, I hung my head and avoided everyone's eyes. Then, above the din outside the galley, I broke the silence. "Mates, maybe we should pray," I said wearily.

No one spoke for a few seconds. Then, one by one, each man nodded. We bowed our heads.

"God," I said, "if you get us to shore, we'll all go to church . . . Amen."

It was a short, irreverent prayer that, in my heart, I directed to my mum's God. It seemed to hit the mark for my mates too.

A memory of a Bible story on the Sunday school flannel board flashed through my mind. Jesus had rebuked a tempest and saved his disciples.

When the blow finally abated, we celebrated our survival, scurrying like ants to repair the mast and sails. But it only took a day for a new peril to surface, and it hit the crew even harder than the cyclone.

For days, our schooner floated in listless doldrums as if frozen in a sea of glass.

Berto informed Audrey that we had little rice to ration. We were nearly out of fresh water, and the *Galaxy's* engine still refused to kick over. Short-tempered and exhausted, our gaunt, sunburnt crew sheltered from the relentless sun wherever we could. As days passed, Berto's menu included an occasional fish divided six ways.

Just when all hope from our desperate prayer seemed unanswered, a sniff of wind began filling our sails. Dean recalculated our course to sail for the island of Mauritius. Sailing at a turtle's pace to avoid more doldrums, we hoped to find land before the weakest among us died of thirst or starvation.

One night, I relieved Cap Audrey after her shift at the helm ended. The smell of gin lingered in the wheelhouse, and I took a compass bearing. I checked and double-checked the direction.

Audrey had reached her stateroom door when she heard my accusation.

"You nutter! You've been sailing the wrong direction. We're off course!"

Cap Audrey spun about. "Not likely," she muttered before reentering the wheelhouse. She shouldered me aside and stared at a map. "We're right where we should be."

I started to argue, but gin had emboldened her, so I left the wheelhouse to report our disagreement to Dean and Mark. They rolled out of their bunks, and we trooped to the wheelhouse to confront our captain. Audrey stormed to her stateroom when Dean and Mark confirmed that I was right.

My "assault" on her navigational skills did not endear me to our captain.

"Mauritius!"

After 26 days of storms, doldrums, and near starvation, we sighted Port Louis, the capital of the island, Mauritius. Our prayers had been answered, which we promptly forgot. We approached the busy wharf at Port Louis under sail without engine—a helmsman's nightmare. Dean threaded a needle between two reefs—one to port and the other to starboard—and hollered to the crew to drop sails and anchor the boat a few feet from the dock—another overlooked miracle.

We tied off the *Galaxy* and gathered our bags, ready to escape our waterlogged prison—until three customs agents climbed aboard.

Out of earshot, Captain Audrey excitedly addressed the officers. We watched the demeanor of the uniformed agents abruptly change. Hands on their pistols, they ordered Mark, Berto, and I to stay on the *Galaxy* to answer charges leveled against us by our captain. Audrey had accused us of mutiny on the high seas!

She alleged that we had violently taken control of her vessel— an offense that, if proved, carried lengthy jail terms in nearly every nation in the world.

Weak from exhaustion, and looking the part of bloodthirsty pirates, we denied the charge, but with little effect. Audrey had longstanding connections in Mauritius, and our defense fell on deaf ears.

Audrey and Dean gave us smug looks as they disembarked, leaving us with the customs agents who grilled us further. Fortunately, I wasn't the only "mutineer" who spoke some Creole. Berto had family and friends in Mauritius. He invited the most senior agent to his galley. In a few minutes, the two emerged, laughing together like old mates.

Berto had shown him Audrey's graveyard of gin bottles and informed the official about her erratic behavior. With a dismissive wave, the agent in charge liberated us, and we left the *Galaxy* forever.

One impossible obstacle remained, and I reminded Mark and Berto.

"We better find Audrey and Dean before they burn our passports…"

As captain of the *Galaxy*, Audrey still held the crew's passports in her possession.

We wandered in and out of shops until we tracked down the mum-and-son duo coming out of a bar. Cap Audrey's accusations hadn't carried enough weight to land us in a Mauritius jail after all. They gave up our passports without a fight.

Mark, Berto, and I agreed that we had one glaring obligation to answer before renting a room and drinking away bad memories. I glanced across the street where an ornate Catholic church cast a beam into our souls. Inside, we stood before an icon of Jesus on his cross, pain wracking his face.

Berto knelt, and I said aloud, "God. Thank you." My two friends grunted affirmation. "If you hadn't saved us, we'd be dead. You kept us alive. We know that."

I waited for a robed priest to swish into the sanctuary and bless us, or perhaps for God's voice to acknowledge our gratitude. But nothing spiritual happened. It was like my Anglican experience all over again. Empty.

Days later, I parted with Mark and Berto and hitched a ride to Tamarin Bay, where I fit hand-in-glove with a free-living Creole culture. For months, diving and surfing in Mauritius filled my calendar, while my restless soul yearned for some rationale for living.

CHAPTER 4

REALMS OF DARKNESS AND LIGHT

Guilt

With tattered sails, the *Galaxy* **had limped into the harbor in** *Mauritius, an island off the east coast of Africa. My ill-fated 26-day voyage aboard the schooner* **had ended. And thanks to our galley cook's liaisons, I escaped jail time for the alleged crime of mutiny.

I immediately understood why Mark Twain wrote that "heaven was copied after Mauritius." For two months, I surfed along the white beaches and hiked trails winding through billowing cane fields and eucalyptus forests. In the company of fellow divers, I immersed my mind in the distinctive Creole culture—and smoked hashish to numb the lack of purpose I felt as I recuperated from my ordeal at sea.

Surfing has been called "a sport that is part swimming, part skiing, part skydiving, and part Russian roulette . . . " For me, the only endeavor that rivaled surfing was descending *beneath* the waves to explore and hunt sea creatures (and sometimes *be* hunted).

In Mauritius, Simone, a descendant of slaves and a Creole diving virtuoso, showed me secret surfing spots, like One Eyes and Souillac, along the nearly 100 miles of shoreline.

My Creole host taught me how to dive at night with a spotlight to disorient spiny lobsters and parrotfish hiding in coral reefs. The bright light "hypnotized" fish and crustaceans, making them easy prey. Simone and his family supplemented their income by harvesting the sea bounty. They sold all manner of sea creatures to wealthy patrons and swanky restaurants in nearby tourist hotels.

Simone, Creole Diver

Among my new diving friends, I still paraded as a godless intellectual who wandered the choicest, most seductive, and vicious environments on earth in search of ultimate knowledge. But deep down, I knew that I was no closer to uncovering the purpose for my existence than when I left New Zealand.

My dramatic "cruise" aboard the *Galaxy* had shaken my self-confidence, and my prayers had touched "God." He had saved me from starvation and death at sea—*unless it was simply bonne chance* (good luck).

In the evenings, when the red-rimmed sun dipped beneath the horizon, I mulled over the big questions of life. A theater of stars above

Tamarin Bay dominated the nights, and I wondered: *Did all this stunning beauty burst into existence by accident—and how can I know which god created it?*

Evidence of a higher power shaped the culture of Mauritius: hundreds of Hindu shrines to Lord Shiva and Rahda Krishna; mosques for Mohammed; statues of Vishnu and Ganesh (the elephant god); temples to Choisan (the Chinese god of wealth); as well as dozens of Buddhist shrines. Devotees celebrated festivals corresponding with their images and deities.

In Mauritius, was I nearer to discovering true deity? Had my Asiatic roving finally delivered me to a power beyond the effete "Christianity" that my mother cherished?

My rock-hard shell of atheism had softened, and I was open to religious discovery as never before. Lolling in a hash-stupor, friends and I sometimes discussed the tenets of their faith as well as Christianity. The Creoles assumed that I was a Christ-worshiper because of my white skin. I hid the truth—that I surfed on waves of doubt without a leg rope.

My vicars in New Zealand had drummed the Ten Commandments into my head. On Mauritius, I could no longer hide from my conscience. I seldom communicated with my girlfriend Kerry back in New Zealand, and guilt over my immoral lifestyle would overshadow all of my relationships when I returned home.

A religious ceremony known as "Cavadee" mirrored the way my wounded conscience felt:

Clouds of incense engulfed hundreds of Hindu worshipers in the streets, many wearing brightly colored saris. Each family carried a bamboo arch, a Cavadee, festooned with flowers and peacock feathers. Two pots of milk were lashed to the Cavadee framework, and worshipers delivered the milk to a temple to appease Muruga, their Hindu god. In a procession to the temple, devotees confessed sins and repented.

As proof of their devotion, true believers pierced their backs, chests, tongues, and cheeks with silver needles. Some dragged carts tied to cords with hooks bored through their flesh. Priests ambled among the throng tugging and twisting the needles, further wounding the penitents.

Should I join the pilgrimage of Mauritians marching in the Tamil (Indian) festival of forgiveness? It was customary for pilgrims to welcome spiritual "companions" into their souls as they shuffled in a tranced state. They craved absolution and cleansing of conscience. Participating in Cavadee was a Mauritian's ultimate act of purification and contrition.

I watched the procession with the belief that I had strayed too far from *any* god to expect forgiveness.

FAMILY TIES

Among boarders, a surfer earned gravitas by conquering legendary breaks. I had never surfed the notorious Jeffreys Bay on the heel of South Africa—known for shark attacks and its unpredictable, violent combers. Jeffreys Bay had been featured in the intoxicating movie, *Endless Summer.* That film inspired me to abandon good sense—and a lucrative career—over a year ago.

And I wasn't the only surfer who dreamed about a magical "endless summer." Rich blokes (we called these novice surfers "grommets") flew to J-Bay to surf epic swells with names like Kitchen Windows, Supertubes, Boneyards, and Impossibles. A skilled surfer might ride Supertubes for nearly a quarter mile, and if waves lined up, the trip could last for half a mile!

During months of carousing in Mauritius, I had exhausted my traveling funds and my supply of hashish. After barely scraping up enough money for an airline ticket, I flew to Durban, South Africa. I easily found a lucrative job at the Umhlanga Sands Hotel at Umhlanga Rocks—teaching waterskiing and scuba diving.

By surfing my way south, I hit killer breaks at Cave Rock and Coffee Bay before reaching the surfers' paradise of Jeffreys Bay. I was killing two grand adventures with one flight. I surfed the most acclaimed, gorgeous breaks in the world, *and* I realized my dream of seeing elephants, rhinos, and lions in the Hluhluwe-Imfolozi Game Reserve in the region of KwaZulu-Natal, South Africa.

My safari on the South African savannah fulfilled a dream and revived my longing for home. I ruminated over the contrast between my safe, hospitable New Zealand and the bloody savagery of Africa. Conflict in my soul aroused a heightened spiritual vigil—a restlessness soon quenched by a chain of miracles. The kick-off to a beyond-natural spectrum of deadly events began in April of 1982.

A letter from my younger brother, Neil, living in Perth, Australia, caught up with me in Mauritius shortly after my sojourn in South Africa. The invitation to his wedding (to be held at Thames in New Zealand) tossed a spanner into my self-centered plans. I had hoped to explore more ocean splendors with my Creole brothers. A mystical "something" that I craved still eluded me, and I had even mapped out a trek through the heart of Africa to Europe to find it.

I hated to admit it, but my father's oracle was as good as gold after all. I had wasted my academic degree *and* drained my future of prime opportunities. If I returned home to New Zealand, I would have nothing to show for nearly two years of seeking a nonexistent "perfect wave."

I dutifully decided to fly to Australia via Reunion and Mauritius to catch up with my brother in Perth before heading back to New Zealand.

While in Mauritius on the way home, Simone interrupted my mission.

He showed up at my door lit up like mellow moonlight. Sensing the burden that I carried at leaving Mauritius for New Zealand, he pleaded with me to night-dive with him one last time . . .

Creoles call a close shave with death *bonne chance* (good luck), and my luck felt threadbare. I had cheated death time and time again, but nothing in my past could prepare me for the rarified odyssey God had in store.

Near Night Diving

ONE LAST DIVE

"Nah, nah, nah, Simone. I canna' go with you tonight, bro. What about the storm? See it there?"

Simone and I stood on my balcony at a bungalow I shared with two other surfers. It was nearing midnight, and he was already dressed in his wetsuit. He held flippers under one arm and gestured with his hands, trying to wash away my doubts.

"No problem, Ian! We go five miles down the coast. The storm—she's passing by, man. *Nous serons bien* [We'll be fine]!"

A shiver ran through me. I recalled the feel of flesh ripping on jagged coral, and I pictured Simone's wooden skiff grinding on a reef. Only months ago, I had survived a merciless cyclone aboard the *Galaxy* in the Indian Ocean . . .

A flash of lightning illuminated Simone's infectious grin—I hated to disappoint my diving brother. But it was irrational to dive during a lightning storm. At times, the ocean was a massive conductor of electricity. As a lifeguard back home, I had often cleared shorelines of swimmers when an electrical storm approached.

Simone's voice grew quiet and serious. "Ian, brother. Tonight, I take you to the most amazing reef you ever see! I got the spear guns in the boat and . . . "

I raised my hands in surrender.

One last dive, I thought. *I might never come back to Mauritius, and if Simone believes that the storm is moving out to sea, I can trust him. This is a once-in-a-lifetime dive! Think of it. Being present when a tempest washes sea creatures toward a reef. Who knows what strange sights the squall might send inland while we harvest fish for Simone's family?*

I grabbed my dive bag and underwater diving torch.

INVISIBLES

For five miles, the cadence of distant thunder blended with Simone's oar strokes and the symphony of lapping waves. Simone rowed with one oar. His friend Eric, a long-time diving companion, rowed with the other. A shirtless boy, about 14—whom I assumed was Eric's little brother—hugged himself to keep warm. Silently, he studied us, listening to us josh and banter while I sat in the stern, keeping a pushing pole from rolling about.

We had been floating parallel the shore for several minutes when Simone held up his hand. Oars stopped clattering. I estimated we were half of a mile from shore where a wide submerged reef stretched between the beach and us.

My beam of light revealed a magical coral kingdom beneath us. At varying depths, colonies of orange, pink, and white mushroom-shaped polyps beckoned to us with their wavy appendages. Sea nettles, sponges, and cream-colored invertebrates populated living flowerbeds. Gargoyle-looking fish froze, as in a theater spotlight, when our torches penetrated their sea castles.

Creole Fishermen with Ian

Our boat boy enviously watched us sort through diving gloves, snorkels, masks, and flippers. Simone and his friend wore full-body wet suits. I wore a less restricting "shorty" that left my forearms bare. I staked out a ridge of coral sloping sharply into a dark abyss and accepted the challenge to descend as far as my lungs would permit. Simone and his friend roved purposefully away from the boat, probing a beautiful coral grove.

I swam in an environment as alien to the human body as outer space. I remembered my Uncle Rex—when I was an impressionable lad—spinning tales of his diving adventures in the Pacific Islands. Every couple of years, my father's brother, Rex, reentered our lives bearing gifts of seashells and artifacts he had collected on his dives around the Solomon Islands.

Would I be diving in Mauritius if it wasn't for untamed Uncle Rex and his tantalizing stories? I wondered.

I surfaced for a few seconds, postponing my reverie, and gulped air several yards from the skiff. I propelled myself under again, aiming to investigate crevasses that looked promising for spiny lobster—but quickly forgot my objective. From the direction of open water, my spotlight touched a ghostly form slowly angling toward me.

It appeared to be a translucent, bell-shaped "head" with several fingerlike tendrils trailing from its form. No features adorned its glassy interior, and I couldn't help myself. I reached out my gloved hand as it approached within inches of my diving torch and clenched the gossamer substance into my palm. The gauzy invertebrate squished through my fingers like jelly and fled into the darkness away from my light. I had never seen a box-like creature quite like it before.

The storm must have washed it inland, I thought.

I was about to resume my hunt for crustaceans when I gasped. A jolt in my forearm—unlike a typical scrape from coral—struck me with the force of a 220-volt electrical main.

I flashed my torch wildly, stroking my enflamed right forearm, and the hard rubbing numbed the pain. In the light from my torch, I detected no jaw marks or cuts—only angry red streaks against my white skin. I grabbed my fear by the throat—a skill acquired from hundreds of life-threatening occasions—and momentarily overpowered my rising concern. I didn't want my mates to remember how "fainthearted Ian" had spoiled their spectacular dive. I decided to grab a lobster or crayfish on my way up to the boat . . .

I pointed my torch briefly into the abyss and *froze*. Two more translucent, box-like invertebrates—akin to the one I had carelessly squished in my fingers—floated past. One of the creature's flowing tentacles brushed across my injured right forearm before I could jerk it away.

I fought the impulse to rip off my mask and scream, and it was a peculiar time to think about my allergies (as a boy, I swelled up like a balloon from a single bee sting).

Tonight, two box jellyfish had lashed my forearm.

I had no idea that the sting from one box jellyfish (also known as a sea wasp) could kill a diver within minutes if stung above the shoulders. My only hope was antitoxin—sitting in a dilapidated hospital fifteen miles away. A deadly countdown had commenced with my life ebbing away in increments of encroaching paralysis.

I popped my head through the lagoon's surface where light from my torch reflected the reef in vivid florescence. I moaned when I spied the silhouette of the child against a dark sky several yards away. It might as well have been a mile to Simone's skiff. I kicked with my fins and dogpaddled with my good hand, dragging my throbbing right arm. Then the unthinkable happened.

What felt like stringy kelp skimmed across the back of my wetsuit and grasped my right forearm like gentle fingers. I thrashed in panic, ripping translucent threads from my already swollen limb. I had been stung by a sea wasp a third time.

Shreds of severed tentacles floated off. I cradled my semi-paralyzed arm with the other arm, breathlessly clasping the shaking torch. I trained a beam toward the abyss, and all the expletives I knew fell short of expressing my terror. My torchlight illumined hundreds of undulating box jellyfish. Several surged away from the horde and loomed close to me.

One sting to my face and I'm done for, I thought. *I'll never make it to the skiff.*

Flinging the torch like a shield, I struggled toward the boat, rasping to the curious boy, "Something stung me! Do you know what it is?"

He shrugged a "How should I know?" and pointed to snorkel bubbles roiling in a shoulder-deep pool several feet from the skiff. Simone rose from the pool grinning, holding a spiny lobster in one hand. My light beam reached him before I did.

My best Creole lodged in my throat as I tore off my mask and gestured that I needed to get into the boat. Curious about my clamoring and splashing, Simone stood on a coral shelf, baffled as to why I was spoiling the memorable sendoff he had planned for me.

I ducked underwater, desperately propelling myself with my fins, until a gossamer glint close to my ear stopped me. Instinctively I threw up a hand to protect my face and received a jolt from the tendrils of a *fourth* sea wasp—adding to the mesh of lesions on my injured right arm.

Unsteadily, I mounted the shelf of coral near Simone, and we trained our torches on my wounds. My ravaged appendage had swelled to twice its size and red welts streaked my veins.

Eric still fished somewhere beneath the boat, and the boy watched us, expressionless. An undertow of fear tugged at Simone. His eyes met mine, wordlessly expressing what he believed to be my fate.

"Invisibles..." he said, shaking his head. "*Combien de?* [How many?]"

I held up four shaky fingers. "Quatre, je pense [Four, I think]."

Simone flashed the light on his own face for effect. He held up one finger. "*One* kills you, Ian." He made the sign of a throat being cut.

But how am I standing upright if I'm stung by FOUR "invisibles"?

I detected panic in Simone's voice as he let loose a string of Creole too fast for me to understand—except for the words *"C'est fini"* and "Hospital at Quatre Bornes."

Simon was a native of Mauritius and had been diving for 20 years. I trusted his dire assessment. "*Aller, Aller!* Go! Go!" he nearly screamed.

My right arm was almost completely paralyzed. Simone motioned me to submerge again and maneuvered me to the side of the boat. He climbed into the skiff, crying orders to the boat boy while Eric surfaced, looking curious.

As Simone dragged me over the side of the skiff, excruciating pain turned the whole scene a bleary scarlet. I endured my fifth and last sea wasp sting due to my right forearm's belated entry into the boat.

What have I done to deserve this?

I asked it under my breath—and thought I knew. I tried to shut out multiple questionable occasions flashing across my mind.

Was this payback for the bad things I'd done?

I sat, moaning quietly, in the back of the boat among Simon's lobsters and parrotfish. I could feel the boat glide into a pool of deeper water—then stop. Simone and Eric began swimming and shoving the boat across the jagged outer reef, and I shouted, "Come with me. Get in!" but Simone refused "No, Ian. Too heavy!"

The skiff ground on another ridge of coral, tearing the boat's bow. To damage Simone's boat (which was his means of livelihood) hurt me in a different way. But Simone and Eric never hesitated. They pushed their skiff across shelves of coral, leaving slivers of wood and gouges in their wake.

Abruptly, Simone shoved his boat away and shouted, "The boy can get you in. He'll pole you to shore. Get to the hospital at Quatre Bornes. It's the closest one. *Bonne chance*, Ian!"

ABANDONED?

I focused on the shimmering clouds above me and the heavy, rhythmic breathing of the boat boy poling with all his strength across the reef. Crustacea rattled beneath me as what felt like spiny barbs meandered through my bloodstream. In my right armpit, venom staked a claim to a lymph gland on its way to my right lung.

Struggling to breathe, I forced myself to sit up and strip off my constrictive wet suit. While fumbling to put on shirt and pants, a punch in my kidney warned me that venom had reached it. Sweat poured off my forehead. My tongue and lips dried up like leather.

We were halfway to shore.

I held my panic in check as the toxin pulsated through arteries in my right leg, numbing it. My lifeguard medical training told me that if the toxin reached my heart or brain it could be a fatal terminus. Waves thrust the skiff onto the beach, and the boat boy motioned me to disembark. It took all my concentration to tumble out, and I lay upon the strand like a beached porpoise. The teenager stood with hands on hips looking down at me.

A few seconds passed, and he decided. He glanced toward the two men left behind on the reef and motioned me to wrap my good arm around his shoulder. One of my legs worked fine, but the other functioned intermittently as we stumbled upon the beach away from the skiff.

If I had known which god to thank for the boat boy, I would have been praying. It was well past midnight when he eased me onto the side of the deserted road running along the strand. He tried one last time to help me to my feet, pointing to lights in the distance. Then he ran back toward the skiff saying he wanted to rescue the other divers too.

I knew what he was thinking. He feared the deadly horde of sea wasps gathering near Simone and Eric.

"They'll be okay! They have full-body wetsuits. Please! Get me to the hospital. Or to a telephone..." I pleaded.

But his mind was made up. He dissolved into the darkness. I listened to his pole clump against the boat's stern. In agony, I lay back on the side of the road, watching stars emerge from behind clouds. Simone had been right. The storm had died away—while mine was only beginning.

"WHERE'S MY MONEY, WHITE BOY?"

Sleep. It seemed illogical to relax if I was dying. But the desire for sleep overwhelmed me. I drifted to the edge of comatose repose. My eyelids closed for an instant—then snapped open!

At my shoulder, a powerful male voice spoke to me. "Son, if you close your eyes, you'll never wake up again."

Who was this person so close that I could touch "him?" I kept listening and tried to see him but detected no physical form. *This is crazy,* I thought. *I'm hearing the Invisible Man talk to me!*

With faculties electrified, I determined that the voice had likely interrupted my descent into death. I rolled to my good knee and labored to stand up. By shifting weight from my numb leg to my good one, I limped toward distant streetlights.

Embers from cigarettes grew brighter as I approached three taxicabs in a barely-lit parking lot. Three Indian cabbies stood beside their vehicles, and I mentally petitioned hope when they acknowledged me. They waited impatiently for my dark form to stagger close enough to laugh at.

Drunk?

"No, no! I'm not! I've been stung by *cinq* invisibles! You know! Jellyfish! I need to go to the hospital! I'm dying. You take me. Please! You take me?"

"How much you pay, white boy? We don't work for no money."

I immediately offered to pay them. "Fifty dollars? No, 100 dollars—U.S."

"Okay. You show us money…"

"I don't have any on me, but…"

At my confession, all three cabbies guffawed like hyenas. The drunken white boy had said the wrong thing.

"Look, I *have* money—just not *with* me. Please! I'll pay you."

It wasn't working.

Am I destined to die here because of these heartless cabbies?

In answer to my thoughts, the distinctive voice that had interrupted my comatose slide toward death broke in. *Son, are you willing to beg for your life?*

Looking for the person speaking directly behind me, the flickering streetlights revealed no one. I turned back to the cab drivers. They were moving toward their cars.

"I am willing!"

My thoughts raced.

In this bigoted culture, has anyone ever known a white "boy" willing to beg?

I fell to my knees. I cupped my hands chest-high, glued my eyes on their feet, and implored the cab drivers for help. I watched their feet moving away—all except a single pair in dirty sandals. This cabbie stopped and turned around.

I hoped that I could keep my submissive posture for as long as it took—and I felt a hand reach around my shoulder. He was helping me to the taxi's door!

Without a word, he drove for several minutes in the direction of the hospital. I recognized the terrain that we passed and the village where I lived at Tamarin Bay.

"You stay at Tamarin Bay Hotel, right? Where's my money, white boy?"

"No! I live with Creoles..."

Brakes.

My reluctant chauffeur bumped his taxi against the curb. "I drop you here at hotel. *They* can take care of you—you haven't paid me no money!"

"I promise you! I'll give you all the money I have. But I need to get to the hospital. I'm begging . . . " I had no strength left to convince him.

"Get out!"

"I can't. I can't move my . . . "

"Out!"

He was screaming and leaned over me to wrench open the passenger's door. He buttressed his command by shoving me out. I rolled onto the concrete, barely avoiding his rear tire as he sped away.

Merciless. Nasty. Stinking. This is the world I live in! I ruminated in self-pity as I lay on my belly, shivering and alone. *Earth is hell! Who wants to live here if people treat others this way? I should just do myself a favor and die.*

I scraped up a memory before giving up completely. My grandfather had suffered from breathing mustard gas in World War I, and then he rejoined the New Zealand army to fight in World War II. Some of his last words to me were, "Ian, fight to your last breath. Don't give up . . . "

I hadn't given up. I had soldiered on my whole life—*but here I lay, alone. Wasn't I alone?*

A flashlight grazed me, then it bored into my eyes as I groveled on one elbow to rise. Someone yelled, and I braced for inevitable kicks to the "drunk" trespassing the hotel property. But, instead, a Creole friend materialized, dressed in a security guard's uniform.

Mauritius Hospital

"Ian? Man, what you doin'? I never seen you like this, bro."

Daniel was a strong man. He towered over me, quizzically, trying to fathom my odd behavior. We knew each other well from months of surfing, drinking, and night diving together.

Weakness overwhelmed me, but I managed to pull up my sleeve.

Daniel gasped. "Invisibles," he said in Creole, shining his light on my forearm. He knew.

"You been diving with Simone tonight?"

"Oui," I breathed.

"C'est fini, Ian. [You're finished, Ian.]"

Tamarin Bay Hotel

Shaking his head, he scooped me up and carried me into the dimly lit Tamarin Bay Hotel, owned by three Asian men. Daniel settled me into a rattan chair in the hotel's bar, where the only occupants appeared to be the three owners. The heavy odor of incense and smoke permeated the room. The men barely looked up from their Mahjong tiles when Daniel, with no explanation, whirled and left the way he came!

I am abandoned again, I thought.

The fearless Celtic warrior from Down Under had survived decades of near-fatal adventures, but now I slumped helpless and dying in a dingy island pub. Venom traveled through my bloodstream, leaching into organs and sapping my precious strength.

"I'm dying. I've been stung by five box jellyfish," I slurred, pulling back my sleeve to show off angry red lesions crisscrossing my forearm. I pleaded in my limited Chinese. "Hospital at Quatre Bornes! I need to go."

But the Mahjong players only chuckled together.

The youngest of the three sidled unsteadily near me. He stopped and pointed at my arm. "White boy! See? Heroin no good for you. Old men take opium. Ha, ha . . ."

From the marks on my forearm, he assumed I was an addict! The outrage triggered a seizure of wild convulsions for several seconds. Two of the mirthful hotel owners held me to the chair until my shaking suddenly stopped.

A strange coldness seeped into my bones. From the tips of my toes, I could feel death moving up my body. I shivered like I had finished an ice-cold swim. I pleaded with the hotel owners to get me a blanket.

"Hospital at Quatre Bornes!" I pleaded, catching the eye of the youngest man. "You have a car? Take me, or I die right here. Please..." My voice trailed off to a whisper, and the man shook his head.

"No way, white boy. No take my car. Sorry. We wait for ambulance for you. Don't worry."

More outrage boiled in my heart.

If I'd have had the strength, I would have punched him. I leaned forward and tried to grab his lapel, picturing a satisfying head-butt to his face. But I stopped.

The Voice cut through my anger and saved me again. *Son, the venom is close to your heart. If you hit this man, the adrenaline rush will kill you.*

I mulled over the warning. *Okay, but if I survive this, I will come back and deal with him later.*

As I tried to control my anger, Daniel trotted back through the door. I would have hugged him if I could—he had called for an ambulance.

My Creole angel and another security guard hoisted me out of the chair and half-carried, half-dragged me outside. I tried to suck in a cool breath of air, but only one lung seemed to respond.

An ambulance had been idling in front of the Tamarin Bay Hotel, but it pulled away. Daniel hopped a wall to flag it down.

The ambulance driver had assumed that his dispatch to the hotel was bogus. My lips were too numb and dry to configure a whistle, but Daniel's loud trills caught the ambulance driver's attention. He spun around in a U-turn.

At the curb, the young driver lit a cigarette while Daniel loaded me into the car like a sack of potatoes. An army cot hosted my pain-wracked body, and Daniel slammed the doors shut.

I need to stay awake to tell the doctor that I require antitoxin, I thought as the old Renault revved and climbed a steep hill. My head jostled against the hatchback, and I worried.

Will the venom circulate to my brain quicker because it's slanted downhill?

CHAPTER 5

STAY OR RETURN?

The Lord's Prayer and Mum

At 26, I was proud of my self-sufficiency. I maintained an invisible wall that guarded against heartrending breakups and shipwrecked friendships in my life. I had sealed off my feelings, lest they be trampled.

I routinely ended a relationship if someone got too close to the real Ian McCormack.

But in the back of a jerry-rigged ambulance, my emotions snapped their leash. I longed for reassurance from someone.

Staring at the ceiling of the old Renault ambulance, I beheld images projected upon my consciousness. A blond-haired boy ran carefree along the seashore, then morphed into an adolescent, and then transformed into a teenager. Next, I saw myself as a man at my parents' Waihi beach house...

I wasn't dreaming. My eyes were wide open. I could see lighted buildings as we passed them. The vision in front of me presented my life and relationships at different stages.

I've read about this. Life flashes before the eyes upon death. I'm really dying. Then I scolded myself. *You idiot! You should have never gone diving with Simone . . .*

Words from my lips felt leaden, but my inner thoughts conveyed exactly what I wanted to communicate. I could feel the wretched sensation of fear creeping through me. My heart galloped like a lame horse, and my operational lung inflated and deflated like heaving bellows.

What happens next? I asked myself. *Where will I go if I die? Is there anything out there? Is there life after death?*

All images in my consciousness swiftly vanished, and a final episode played on the screen. Mum knelt beside her bed with her hands clasped in prayer. She looked up and spoke to me, as clear as crystal. "Ian, no matter what you do, or how far from God you find yourself—if you call out to Jesus in your heart, he will hear you. He will forgive you."

The vision of my mother snapped off like a light switch, and darkness smothered me again. A caravan of philosophies tumbled helter-skelter through my mind. *Am I an atheist or an agnostic? Is the venom short-circuiting my brain?*

Mum is the one person in my life whom I trust. Has she shown me the path to find God, after all? Should I pray to my mum's Christian God?

On the day of my confirmation, Mum had pleaded with me to "call out to Jesus in my heart . . . " and now I grasped what she meant. *This* kind of communication was not cerebral. Praying had less to do with my intellect and everything to do with my "heart."

I could barely form a sentence with my lips, but I effortlessly expressed my thoughts and emotions from within a dynamic speech center at the core of my being.

The Lord's Prayer commandeered my thoughts as its verses (Matthew 6:9-13) scrolled across my field of vision.

I wordlessly screamed for help in the ambulance, embracing this prayer as my new coat of arms. At the summit of my anguish, God was unveiling his blueprint for me to receive eternal life.

The words "forgive us our sins" appeared before my eyes. I had crossed the line too many times to expect God's mercy—but Mum had insisted that Jesus would forgive me no matter what I had done! So, I prayed a presumptuous prayer that no one who lived so recklessly should dare.

I bowed my broken heart and said, "Wipe my slate clean, God. I want to start again. Forgive me. Please . . . "

Then another phrase from The Lord's Prayer appeared. "Forgive anyone who has sinned against you."

"You mean the people who have hurt me, betrayed me, and slandered me? I won't hold grudges," I said decisively. "I can forgive them."

But the riveting Voice (easily distinguished from my own) cut through my ego.

Will you forgive the taxi driver who pushed you out of his taxi and left you for dead? And the hotel owners who wouldn't take you in their car to the hospital?

I pondered this. The silence grew unbearable. A heavy mist began drifting across the words of The Lord's Prayer, and I worried that I was losing the blueprint God showed me.

"I'll forgive them! You have forgiven everything I've done. I surely will forgive them," I said—and immediately the fog lifted. My resentments dissolved, and a euphoric sense of wellbeing swept over me—a feeling akin to surfing in triumph on a treacherous wave.

Then four more words from The Lord's Prayer awakened an inner "leap" of joy in my heart that I'll never forget. "Thy will be done." I had no idea the effect that the phrase would have upon me. My submission emanated from the "secret place" of my heart, and inexplicable comfort and assurance saturated me.

I made Jesus's words to his Father my own. I wasn't begging God for survival like I did aboard the *Galaxy*. I entrusted Jesus Christ with Ian McCormack's life, no matter how long or short—God's will, not mine. It was the first time I had ever known true peace—a peace that has never left me for over 40 years.

My choice to receive God's forgiveness, to forgive others, and to submit to God's will birthed a new identity within me. My fear of what came after death (the unknown) vanished—even as my body battled to survive.

And a medical team in Quatre Bornes joined the battle too.

DEAD

At the hospital, a nurse placed a well-used blood pressure cuff on my arm and stared at the gauge for a few seconds. She then smacked it with her knuckle. From my vantage point, it appeared that the mercury was frozen in the glass tube of the machine. The nurse stoically unfastened me and rifled inside a drawer for another monitor. She wrapped another cuff around my upper arm.

The Brits had deeded their military hospital to the Mauritius islanders after World War II.

How many soldiers have these old blood pressure monitors served? I wondered.

The second monitor also registered an absence of blood pressure. She spoke in French—which I barely comprehended. She seemed shocked that I could still draw breath.

In an adjacent room, two men in worn lab coats sat next to one another on a bench. The older, balding doctor jerked awake as the nurse rolled my wheelchair in. The younger, holding a clipboard, yawned and asked my name and address in French—and I ignored him, as my French was very poor.

Locking eyes with the sleepy physician, I hoped he spoke English. I sucked in enough breath to utter, "I'm dying. I've been stung... by *cinq* [five] box jellyfish. I need antitoxin now or I will die in front of you..."

Abruptly, the older doctor stood up. The nurse handed him my sparse medical chart, and his concern mirrored that of the nurse who had read my blood pressure.

He gave the younger doctor a withering glance and studied the lesions on my forearm. The old Mauritius veteran had likely treated all manner of ocean-related wounds and knew that I was dying on his watch.

He shouldered past orderlies and shoved my wheelchair to an emergency room, where he barked orders. A nurse jammed an IV with dextrose into my left arm to abate dehydration, while the doctor gently probed my paralyzed arm.

"Young man, whatever you do, don't close your eyes. We're going to try to save your life. This is antitoxin to counteract the venom. You must fight the poison!"

He handed a syringe full of anti-venom to a nurse. Tightlipped, she plumbed for a vein, shoved the needle in, and depressed the plunger. My blood vessel ballooned, and antitoxin dribbled everywhere except inside my arm. My heart was barely beating. Blood was scarcely moving through my body's arteries, veins, and tissue anymore.

The trembling nurse yanked the syringe free and stuck a second syringe with antitoxin near the same flat vein. The serum bubbled in and barely moved. My doctor forgot I was watching and shook his head ruefully.

Though appearing comatose, I was wide awake throughout the whole fruitless attempt to save me. My eyes never closed. I heard and could see everything and everyone in the room.

"Another one?" the nurse whispered.

The doctor nodded resignedly.

Another nurse, with quivering fingers, massaged the slippery vein, but it appeared to have *collapsed*—like all my other membranes seemed to be doing.

The doctor's voice and demeanor changed to "fatherly." He leaned close to my face and said, "Don't be afraid."

I assumed that this was his prognosis for my death. Orderlies lifted me onto a bed, and the doctor shuffled out of sight. I fought to keep my eyes open, screaming inside, but words would not come out of my mouth.

I instructed my head to turn, but only my eyeballs responded to the mental command. My eyelids fluttered like moth wings as organs inside me shut down. I could *feel* death arriving as the doctor sponged my face one last time before leaving the room. I wanted to call him back again, but my lips wouldn't move. Voices in the room faded, and my eyes felt as if they were sealed shut. My whole body sighed—and in an instant I occupied space *elsewhere*.

ALIVE?

Box jellyfish (chironex fleckeri) swim in schools, and their trailing tentacles are laden with a toxin that paralyzes limbs and destroys the heart and brain. Each tendril can unleash multiple stingers into their prey. I had been stung by *five* box jellyfish (sea wasps), and medical staff at the Mauritius hospital had pronounced me dead. My heart monitor had "flatlined." I could feel the release from my body, as if the battle to stay alive had finished. I was dead physically but still alive. I could see, hear, and feel everything.

In a split second, I was no longer in the hospital but in a place of total darkness.

I still had questions: *If I am deceased, why am I still conscious? Why is my awareness honed to a razor's edge? And why did the doctor turn out the lights?*

I didn't feel dead. My paralysis and pain had vanished. I felt my "essential self" detach from my corpse, and a spiritual me "stood" upright. Disoriented in the utter darkness, I stumbled and reached out for a wall. It was so dark I couldn't see my hand

Gradually, I perceived that I was no longer in the emergency room but had relocated to a cavernous arena somewhere else. The pitch-black arena had a claustrophobic ambience, and I groped for tangible objects here too. I pressed my hand to my cheek, and my fingers passed through as if I was a shadow.

Ian McCormack had vacated his ravaged, flesh-and-blood shell, but he still occupied a spiritual frame—with head, shoulders, torso, arms, and legs.

Fear passed through me when I sensed someone standing close enough to touch me. In fact, a multitude of inmates surged around me. Like me, they seemed to be confused about why they were there. I picked up their conversations and was shocked that some were hearing *my* inner thoughts—though I spoke not a word.

"Shut up! Don't move and don't speak!" one demanded.

Another shrieked, "Stop disrupting us! You *deserve* to be here! Just shut up . . ."

That's exactly what I tried to do. Like a child, I hid in the darkness. I listened to the malevolent, ugly threats around me until I could not endure it a moment more.

"Where am I?" I wailed.

A guttural voice cast back, "You're in hell! Now shut up!"

The insight clung to me like a leech. Hell wasn't at all like I had imagined when I was high on hashish at beach parties.

This can't be hell! Where is the party? It is supposed to be sex, drugs, and rock and roll! Not just total darkness.

Then, I realized you can't have a party when you have no physical body.

How can I feel my body, but when I try to touch it, there's nothing there?

Instantly, I remembered my grandfather telling me how men who had lost their limbs in battle could sometimes still feel them even though they'd been amputated.

Was I actually dead and my physical body was still back in the hospital?

Religion had taught me "hell" was fire and brimstone! Rotting corpses and tormenting demons.

Where is the fire? Why are there no rotting corpses here? Did everyone leave their physical bodies behind when they died?

This darkness could be the "real hell" – no light and no physical body to live out evil desires.

Loneliness permeated this darkness, driving home the awareness that residents here had squandered every opportunity to be somewhere else.

And worst of all was that the offal of remorse soiled every thought. One felt no camaraderie here—only an impending expectation of judgment. This place was a realm where they would be held in "chains of darkness" until the day of judgment when they would be cast into a "lake of fire."

A warped sense of time confused me in this hellish locale. I couldn't tell if I had been there for 10 minutes or 10,000 years. If ever there existed a "kingdom" of darkness, I believed that I had fallen prey to it—and I wanted out.

OUT OF HELL, INTO LIGHT

My taste of this unadulterated despair touched off an avalanche of hopelessness, and I appealed to whomever I had spoken to in the ambulance.

"I asked you to forgive me! Why am I here? 'Thy will be done...' Remember?"

To appoint a measure of time to my next experience fails me.

Suddenly, a brilliant light pierced through the darkness and shone down upon me. As I looked at it, I was lifted up into the light. Rising like a speck of dust caught in the sunlight, I could see a circular-shaped opening like a tunnel high above me. A calming reassurance filled me as I left the darkness and malevolence behind. Pure energy emanated from the aperture ahead. I entered the tunnel feeling weightless and moving at an incredible speed. As white light bathed me, serenity beyond comprehension winnowed through my frame.

From the depths of this shining light, a more intense welcome expressed itself as waves of brilliant light welcomed my approach like heavenly messengers.

The first wave enveloped me with a strong sense of comfort. The second embraced me with tranquility like I had never known.

In the darkness, I had been unable to see my body, but I could feel it was still there. I wondered if I could now see it in the light. Turning to the right, I was amazed to see my arm, hand, and fingers. As I moved them, they responded to my mental command. But they were transparent. No longer flesh and blood but spirit! I realized I had stopped in the tunnel. Eager to see more, I looked back at the source and started moving again.

The third wave of light then enveloped me in wondrous, inexpressible joy. The powerful light radiated unconditional acceptance into my spirit. Laden with emotion, it was undeniably human and relatable.

As I came to the end of the tunnel, my vision was no longer restricted by its circular shape. Light emanated to the extremities of my vision, and I stood at what appeared to be the center of the universe—the place from which the powerful presence originated.

I recalled a Christmas card with simple yet profound words, and its message began to sink in. "Jesus is the light of the world."

In my pursuit of a "perfect wave," I was experiencing "perfect peace." I sensed that the rarest of adventures lay ahead. I felt no rebuke as I sifted through a lifetime of existential wanderings. My questioning seemed to be anticipated...

Two religions dominated Asia: Buddhism and Hinduism. My Buddhist friends taught that destiny was a broken record repeating and repeating with no deity in charge. Hindus worshiped a force that inhabited everything: agriculture, fertility, energy, and environment.

After studying both ideologies, I had chosen a hybrid form of personal atheism as my barcode. I had foolishly constructed a battlement against the Christian God—who now possessed my soul!

IMPOSSIBLE EMPATHY

In the hellish arena, darkness had cloaked my spiritual anatomy from view. But now I gazed at my spiritual body, seeing it as a "being of light." It appeared to be a glowing, lesser reflection of the Greater Light of God.

Standing before what could only be the center of the universe, I wondered. *"Is this just a force in the universe, or is there someone in there?"*

Ian, do you wish to return?

There was no mistaking *that* Voice. I had been worrying that I communed with an impersonal force. But now I realized that a "person" had been listening to my thoughts.

I considered what that meant. The Light, Almighty God, understood me and knew my name…but I didn't tell him my name! I couldn't help but to glance behind me.

Return? To where?

The tunnel leading back to darkness appeared to be fading, perhaps collapsing.

Is this real? Am I dreaming all this?

I remembered lying in the creaky bed at the hospital. I had simply closed my eyes and . . .

Ian, do you want to return?

Yes, I thought without speaking. *But I don't know how…*

In answer to my reckonings, the Voice countered. *If you return, you must "see" in a new light, Ian.*

Are YOU the One True Light?

His answer changed me forever.

Ian, God is Light and in Him there is no darkness at all. (1 John 1: 5)

I could see no darkness in this glorious realm. And as I looked behind myself, there was no shadow, since my transparent body had no physical form to prevent the light from shining through it.

I reflected that I had just come from a kingdom of darkness, and the men there called it hell. I hadn't believed in hell until that point. I thought it was just there to scare people into religion.

And I hadn't believed in God!

But now I understood. I could actually be standing before Him.

I had been living in darkness most of my life, before my heart changing prayer in the ambulance. Then, I was granted pardon and rescued from blindness. I stared in wonder at God Incarnate. He had, for some reason, given me a glimpse of hell—and he now identified himself to me as the True Light.

I whispered aloud, quaking inside, "You *must* be God."

I don't deserve to be here, I thought. *Someone has made a dreadful mistake and brought the wrong man up.*

I stepped away from the Light toward the darkness of the tunnel. I tried to judge myself and hide from His Presence.

Immediately, waves of pure liquid Light washed over me. Wave after wave of pure, unconditional love seized me in a father's tender grip. I had known love from my mother when I was a child. I had known love from my dad when we hunted and fished together. I believed that true love might someday come from intimacy with a good woman—but God's love held me like a vice. His cleansing, healing love surged through me and unlocked the door of my soul—which then opened wide to receive more.

My inhibitions fell away, and I began recounting my offenses to God.

He stopped me. *Ian, in the ambulance, I forgave all your sins when you prayed the Lord's Prayer. Remember? Your heart is totally clean now.*

My fear of judgment evaporated, and I wept like a child.

A longing to step closer to the Light overwhelmed me, and I detected no barrier between God and myself. In faraway lands, self-proclaimed gurus and priests had failed to place a roadmap to universal Truth in my hands. But now the Meaning of Life and the Truth stood a single stride away.

I reached deeply for all the courage I could muster. Then I asked one more question in my mind. *I'm so weary of searching. Can I see you face to face? Can I come into your Light?*

In keeping with my lifelong passion for risk, before I heard him answer, I stepped into Truth's welcoming effluence.

Stepping into this incredible light, I felt it was like entering a cloud of glory, which began to heal my "broken heart." I wept again, not from sorrow, but an emotion I'd never felt before in my life.

The veils of light parted. Standing before me, in all His Glory, stood what had to be God! It was as though He had made a garment out of the cloud of Glory I had just walked through. Lustrous facets of diamond-like stars glistened from his long, white robe. And the closer I came to him, the more rejuvenated I felt.

He had the appearance of a man with His arms outreached in welcome. His long, white hair reached down to His shoulders. Light emanated from His countenance, many times brighter than anything I'd previously seen. It had the intensity of laser light, but it gave off acceptance and love. As I looked into His face, it seemed as though the entire universe could have originated there. It was like looking into eternity within eternity. If He spoke, I could imagine galaxies and constellations coming forth into being!

I questioned the vision before me. *Is that Jesus? I know it is God. But is Jesus God?* Jesus had brown hair, not white hair!

I'd never read a Bible at that point. So, I didn't know that the hair of Jesus was white as snow, and the hair of His head was like pure wool (Revelation 1:13–18). That He is the alpha and omega, the beginning and the end. He is the exact representation of the invisible God. When you've seen Jesus, you have seen the Father. They are ONE.

In awe, I began to walk closer to Jesus. Waves of light came forth from His face as He imparted His Purity and Holiness into me, for *me* to savor!

My inner Ian had been tainted by moral dissipation. Aboard the *Galaxy*, I had dipped my toe into true humility, but now I waded into God's forgiveness. I wept openly over my ignorance.

I stepped into His presence as His arms reached for me. His face, still featureless to my eyes, glowed with indescribable brightness. It seemed fitting to affix his visual eminence to the words, "In the beginning, God created the heavens and the earth."

I've found Almighty God, I thought.

And I sensed that Jesus was pleased to have been found by Ian McCormack.

I used to say, "Unless He appears to me, I won't believe He is real."

And there I was, not only seeing Jesus but speaking with him!

I yearned to see the human features of Jesus's face, but an intense veil of radiance attended him everywhere He moved. I tried to see his eyes, until I was distracted by activity behind him. He stepped aside.

Before me, something like a door stood open. On the other side, my eyes met a fresh new world. Green pastures and lush orchards under blue skies thrilled the farm boy in me. A crystal-clear river wound through a deep-green forest, and upon this living tapestry, the Creator had embroidered colorful flowers. In the distance, a succession of endless mountains kindled my desire to see what lay beyond them.

This is paradise, my home.

I had no idea that God had created a New earth and a New heaven? (1 Peter 3:10-18)

I expected Jesus to shepherd me into the unsullied splendor. Instead, he stepped in front of the entrance. *Ian, now that you have seen, do you want to remain here? Or do you wish to return?*

I needed to decide. Eternity tugged at me like a powerful tide.

How can I leave this? I thought. *I have no wife to shed tears over me. Back home peace has eluded me.*

Then I spoke to Jesus aloud. "You are the only person who loves me just as I am. I want to stay with you. My search for Truth led me here. Why would I go back? No one loves me like you do, and I love no one enough to leave this Paradise."

I resolutely fixed my eyes on Jesus—but my resolve was about to change. Jesus reminded me that I was wrong. He wasn't the only one who loved me unconditionally.

I was about to bid my earthly life goodbye once and for all. As I looked back one last time to say "goodbye cruel world," my Mum appeared in a vision. She looked straight into my eyes, and empathy overcame my desire to stay.

As a young man, I had disregarded my mother's faith when she spoke of heaven and hell. But her persistent prayers had melded God's sovereignty and my stubbornness into divine action. Five of God's ignoble invertebrates had humbled me.

I imagined my mum's grief when she heard that I had been killed…

She will claim my casket at the airport, believing that she failed to lead me to Christ before my death. That would break her heart! Would the trauma cripple her faith? Would her health fail?

Mum needed to know about my deathbed acceptance of Christ.

"God, I need to return to my body for the sake of one person—my mum," I said through tears. "I need to tell her that her prayers worked! What she believes is true! There is a hell, and Jesus is the "Door" to heaven through whom everyone must enter."

The most selfless decision I've ever made was returning to earth—but I can't take a bow for it. Jesus infused me with the kind of love for Mum that he felt for me.

And Jesus had another surprise in store. As I looked back again, I recognized my father standing beside Mum. And behind Dad, stood my brother and sister. Then I saw my friend Jack and a sea of humanity reaching out of sight. Multitudes of people I'd never met in my life.

I asked God why He was showing me all these people.

He answered me. *Ian, most of these people will never step foot inside a church to hear my name. I want you to go back and tell them what you have seen.*

I responded, "But I don't know these people, and I don't love them! I can truly say I love my mother and want to return for her."

He answered me again. *Ian, I love them. And I desire all of them to come to know Me.*

Immediately, my orientation changed in ways I would have never thought possible. I began to see the crowd behind Mum with "fresh" eyes of love.

How do I go back into my body? I wondered.

I needn't have asked.

Jesus said, *Ian, tilt your head. Feel the liquid drain from your eyes. Now, open your eyes and see.*

Instantly I was back in my body!

The table where I lay was cold. Among the medical staff in the room, I was no longer the center of attention. IVs had been detached from my arms. Nurses unhurriedly went about preparing a corpse for storage—*my* corpse.

RETURNING

Before I left New Zealand for my two-year adventure of self-discovery, my mother worried that something tragic might happen to me. My levelheaded father had challenged my hippie defiance differently. He warned me that I was squandering my education and wasting time. He had raised me to be "smarter than that."

Before I left for my OE, my grandmother had quietly invited me to the home that Dad built them behind our bach at Waihi Beach. She wanted to talk. Her and my grandfather's lives had been turned upside down by two world wars, and my grandmother summed up how she felt about my plans to travel.

96 • NIGHT DIVE TO HEAVEN

Guest House   Waihi Beach

Grandparents

"Ian, if you don't see the world now, there might not be anything left to see. Someone is bound to put his finger on the button and blow everything up."

The elder McCormack fully expected the world to end in a holocaust, and I departed with her blessing. I had left all my earthly possessions with family in Hamilton, while my mum prayed for my safe return.

On the table at the hospital in Quatre Bornes, I tried to focus on the physician's hand touching my right foot. He appeared to be holding a scalpel. I lay on my back, and he jabbed my arch, instinctively glancing at my face.

He had pronounced me deceased more than 15 minutes before, so his brown hue went chalky white when I turned my head to the right and opened my eyes. When life animated my fingers and toes, he leapt back in fright. Nurses shrieked as they fled the room in terror. A corpse had just come back to life!

A familiar Voice said, *I have given your life back, Ian.* I felt God's presence by my side while my Indian doctor regained composure.

Moments of astonishment and conversations passed among the medical staff.

"We couldn't save you! We've done nothing to bring you back to life! You were dead for 15 or 20 minutes. Clinically deceased, Son," he finally ventured.

During this conversation, a longing in his eyes asked about his own destiny.

I lay there grappling with reality. God had obviously put me back in my body, but I discovered I was paralyzed from the neck down! That was unbearable to me! I prayed to God, asking Him to heal my physical body or to please take me back to heaven where I'd been. Over the next few hours I felt power like electricity going up and down my body. Despite all the lethal poison that had been in my system I was now completely healed and able to walk out of the hospital the very next day!

CHAPTER 6

THE CALL

Break Out

I describe the next episode in my life from the viewpoint of a 26-year-old unchurched intellectual. I was a recovering atheist who had never uttered words like "saved," "grace," or "believe," acquired from a biblical lexicon. I was a blank page spiritually, untouched by religious doctrines, except for particles of Anglicanism.

Nevertheless, I was a Christ follower who *knew* God's voice. (The same incandescent Truth that "spoke" into my consciousness at 26 has never ceased to illuminate my life some 40 years later).

My friend Simone "broke me out" of the Quatre Borne Hospital. Simone was one of the first faces I awakened to see on the morning after my death-to-life experience. He wasn't smiling. He and a friend had snuck through a hospital window to gain entrance to my room.

They mumbled uncomfortably as they encouraged me to walk out of this dingy hospital corridor. "We get you out of dees place. It smells like a long drop!"

I initially objected to the rescue, but they insisted that they would take care of me. They pushed past orderlies who tried to stop us and stuffed me into a waiting taxi.

"You comin' too?" the driver asked Simone.

Simone studied me for a few seconds, like I was a fish that he wished he could throw back. Then, he showed the taxi driver his palms.

"No, man," he said quietly.

Simone's loyalty to me had its limits—and now he questioned his involvement with an "undead" person. He rattled off my address to the cabby and watched the taxi leave.

At my bungalow, several mates had gathered. They dropped me onto my bed and partied in my living room as I fitfully slept to the wicked beat of hash-sated drummers.

Veteran missionaries report that the spiritual curtain separating the unseen world from the natural world seems "thinner" in Asian countries than in the West. In the West, evil spirits breach this curtain less brazenly, perhaps due to its heritage of Christianity.

But in Asia, on islands like Mauritius, merciless spiritual agents (through voodoo, idolatry, and shamanism) manipulate my Creole brothers and sisters.

In the following days, I experienced this manipulation firsthand. I encountered the rage of demonic agents, furious at losing one of their most useful slaves—me.

NIGHTS OF DEMONS

At the bungalow, I wondered. *Why am I terrified?*

I awoke sweating and shaking in my bed. I clawed at my mosquito netting, straining to see in the dark. The bedroom was pitch black, but from outside an open window, glowing eyes peered at me. Tinted red and narrow like the eyes of a snake, they never blinked but followed the rise and fall of my erratic breathing. I could see they had a darkened, humanlike form.

The party in the living room had died to woozy meditations, so I could clearly hear frightful whispers drifting across my bedroom. They came from the eyes.

"You belong to us, Ian. We are coming back for you."

I grabbed my torch and pointed it at the eyes, but they disappeared.

All I could think to say was "No, you're not!"

I waited in the thickening silence. Had I really just seen "demons?" Was I hallucinating?

God? What's going on?

I called to mind the last two days. My death-to-life odyssey defied description, but every scene felt vividly inscribed upon my brain.

"How do I defend myself from these evil spirits, Lord?" I asked.

Remember your prayer to me in the ambulance?

The Lord's Prayer!

I latched onto each liberating phrase until I came to the wondrous words "…and deliver us from the evil one."

I "read" it again. When I spoke the phrase aloud, a sense of calmness and courage filled my heart.

Turn the lights off, Ian.

I had switched on every light in the room to brighten away the demonic eyes. I took a deep breath. *If I don't shut this light off, I'll never be able to sleep in a dark room again.*

Darkness wrapped me like a blanket, and the room emptied of everyone but God and me. God's presence had created an environment toxic to evil. I slept like a baby the rest of the night, clueless that I had received my first lesson in spiritual warfare. (Ephesians 6:10–18)

The following night, the apparitions kept their promise. They returned. This time, they appeared to be inside my bedroom. Despite my initial fears (I didn't dash to the light switch this time), peace flooded my heart. Gradually, fear turned to courage as I grasped a powerful truth that every believer can claim as their birthright. Greater is Jesus, who abides in us, than the devil or his minions. Satan cannot possess territory where God resides. I switched on the light, and my kneeling posture became a linchpin for my newfound faith. and prayed out loud the Lord's prayer. Peace again enveloped me.

In the morning, my comrades trooped into the bungalow for breakfast after hitting the surf. We bantered (they somewhat warily). What immediately struck me was that I could hear their thoughts like speech. I was troubled as to what was happening to me.

The Lord said, "You are hearing their hearts, Ian. True speech comes out of one's heart."

I retreated to my room to process it.

You're seeing things in a new light, Ian.

It was happening, and I had two more days in Mauritius before I left the island. I couldn't wait to fly out.

The next night, while drifting in a half-slumber, I heard tapping on my window. I shook myself awake and listened. Yes, there was *tapping*.

"Ian, I want to talk to you. Let me in, okay?" a plaintive female voice lilted through my bedroom.

A young, attractive Creole woman I knew stood outside. Some of her friends were asleep in the living room, and I unlocked the back door.

Before I could react, the woman shoved the door wide enough for me to gaze fearfully into her red-tinted eyes.

"Ian," she said in exquisite King's English, "you are coming with us tonight."

I had never heard this woman speak any language but Creole, and she pushed the door wider as I braced to close it. I could barely hold the door against her forceful strength.

Footsteps! Are there others like her coming?

From deep in my fledgling Christian heart, I cried aloud, "In Jesus's name! GO!" The possessed woman's grip on the door went limp. She flew backwards onto the ground as if a powerful force had hit her, and I slammed the door shut and locked it.

But it wasn't the last that I saw of that evil emissary . . .

On my last night in Mauritius, I dozed and waited for a taxi to take me to the airport. I awoke to a clinking sound. I had left a window slightly open for air, and I realized that someone was throwing pebbles at the glass.

It was her again.

I intended to leap up and lock the window, but I was too late. An arm shoved it fully open.

"Ian, we want to talk to you. Come out!"

We?

I recognized the same sultry voice that emanated from the Creole woman the night before. Rocks kept pelting the window, and the woman's voice grew furious.

"Ian! Come out!"

I looked up to see a spear being thrust through the window towards me. As I cried out to the Lord for help, He told me to use my diving torch. Shining it at the window, I could see the red eyes shining out of one the Creole men who was holding the spear. I yanked the weapon from the grasp of the assailant and thrust it back through the window before fastening the latch. I could make out three Creole men and the woman from the night before. All of their eyes were full of this red evil.

Many I knew in the village practiced voodoo. My torchlight dispersed figures outside as they blended with shadows.

I never dozed off again as I waited for the taxi—*that never arrived!* According to the cab company, "someone" had punctured its radiator the night before.

In my bedroom, I sat with my duffel bag on my lap. Unnerved, I waited for another cab from a community several miles from the bungalow. Creole folk in town were up early doing morning tasks—but so were my spiritual prowlers. They stoked rumors of a white surfer who had been killed and reanimated by vile spirits.

Fear had set the villagers' superstitions ablaze. From inside my locked bungalow, I watched the next cabby arrive. He shook his head at a group of Creoles carrying clubs and almost drove away.

Fortunately, I was able to get the taxi to take me to the airport. Then, I flew back to New Zealand via Australia.

To any practicing free-thinking-intellectual-atheist, a nightmare had come true. The Spirit of Jesus had moved into the core of my being. The day I flew out of Mauritius, I had no understanding of the words "born again," but I *felt* new. Old yearnings had been removed from my inner man.

Supertramp roared in my earphones, and I switched off my Walkman. Ocean stretched for miles beneath the plane, and I dived inward.

God? Everything is changing. I don't need to surf anymore. No more hash, Lord. I don't even want to chase girls. What's happening to me?

You are a Christian, Ian. You've been born again.

I knew that voice—it resonated with the same timbre that I remembered from our conversation in the ambulance. It was the same voice I heard while dying on the side of the road.

This voice emanated from the light-infused person who instructed me to return to my lifeless body at the Quatre Borne Hospital. The voice pealed like mellow thunder, and it *felt* audible. I even glanced behind me.

The rest of my flight I "talked" with the Creator of the Universe. I basked in an inexplicable happiness—a foreign sensation that I would later call by its biblical name: "the joy of the Lord."

I deplaned in Perth, Australia for a short visit with my brother to offer congrats on his upcoming marriage. I excitedly told Neil about my journey from death-to-life, and he worried that his big brother had lost his mind.

Staying in his flat in Perth, once again I awoke to voices taunting me. The demons applied the same modus operandi their cohorts used in Mauritius, including shining eyes in the darkness. But strangely these demons' eyes were white!

Quite by accident, I stumbled upon a "summons" that these demonic miscreants answered. My brother's flat-mate owned a spiritual beacon that invited evil. On his fireplace hearth, a benign-looking ceramic Buddha sat cross-legged and grinning at me.

The Lord told me, "The white eyed demon came out of this idol."

I applied the name of Jesus and the only scripture I knew—The Lord's Prayer—to rout the spiritual agents. Then, I packed up and left for Auckland via Melbourne and Sydney.

UNBELIEF AND DISBELIEF

The Ian whom my parents and Kerry hugged farewell was not the man smiling and waving on the tarmac in Auckland. Mum cried when she saw me. Dad shook my hand. Kerry's embrace lingered. I felt a true and loving welcome—until the ride home to Hamilton.

A few miles down the road, my father cut to the chase. "So, Ian? You must have some incredible stories. You've been away for two years. Tell us, what was your most memorable adventure?"

I paused in the waiting silence, not for effect, but to search for a way to begin my strange story.

"I don't know how to explain it, really, Dad. But... I died and came back to life. I saw Jesus! I'm a born-again Christian now."

This was Ian's greatest adventure?

Kerry fixed her eyes on traffic. Unbeknownst to me, she had also given her life to Christ.

Was I was mocking her?

Mum stared into my soul. As an Anglican, she seldom (if ever) heard the words "born again." But her ears perked up when she heard me say "Christian..."

Was Ian joking?

For my father, the impact of my words kicked like a 12 gauge. He paused for a few seconds while everyone listened.

Dad was a professional, a Freemason and a master planner. In advance of his death, he had chosen a casket to be carried by Freemason brethren. My father ferociously guarded his reputation—and his eldest son disappointed him once again.

Then Dad broke the silence, roaring like a boar whose heart felt the touch of steel. "Ian! I never *ever* want you to talk about that again...!"

I shared his pain. The same evil I had encountered in Mauritius and Perth sat in my dad's car. It wasn't my beloved father who fumed, but a caricature of the man I loved.

Dad had more to say to the son he hadn't seen for two years, the son who had squandered his degree and career. A son who couldn't care less about the McCormack name...

My heart ached. Mum changed the subject.

In my bedroom back home, I entered a surreal time warp. Thanks to Mum, all my surf posters remained tacked to the walls. After a few hours of sleep, once again, I awoke in the crosshairs of evil.

In my own bed! In my mother's house?

The demonic entities evidently tracked me across oceans. My anger erupted in audible curses as I recognized the same ugly presence that I encountered in Mauritius. I did not realize that they were most likely local spirits, not ones that followed me all the way from Mauritius.

After a few untargeted outbursts, I followed up with, "Out! Get out! Help me, Jesus. Father, who art in heaven...."

And somewhere during the Lord's Prayer that I quoted at the top of my lungs, the room completely emptied of the evil presence.

"I'm so sick of these demons, Jesus. How do I get rid of them for good?"

Read the Bible, Ian.

Could it be that simple? No rituals? No invocations? No chants? Just reading the Bible?

"But I don't have one, Lord."

Your father does.

I'm not sure how long Dad had been listening to me jab epithets at the devil, but he stood frowning in the hall in bare feet and pajamas.

"Are you off your noggin? What are you doing?"

"Just a bad dream, Dad. G'night..."

I closed the bedroom door gently, conjuring up the real "nightmare" of asking my father for his Bible.

Ask him...

God's decree wasn't open for discussion. I knocked on Dad's bedroom door.

He was still awake, but Mum was fast asleep, until he groused, "Ian's here. He wants a Bible to read!"

After a discussion about where Dad's Bible nested in his closet, he fished out the Bible he used for Masonic rituals.

"Thanks."

I carried the big King James to my room, leaving my parents to wonder what imposter had replaced their eldest boy.

"In the beginning God created the heavens and the earth . . . "

I read most of Genesis until my eyelids drooped toward sleep—and a wondrous affirmation soaked into my dreams. In the Bible, God was speaking to me about his creation and light.

I really *was* seeing everything in a new, eternal light—and it was only the beginning. There were 65 more books in God's Word waiting for me to explore.

In the coming weeks, my family called my hunger for scripture an obsession. Dad even offered me money and his car to check out local pubs, but I couldn't tear myself away from reading. Mum suggested that I get reacquainted with friends that I hadn't seen for two years. But my fascination with scripture continued to grow like New Zealand wheat. Days turned to weeks as the Word of God put meat on the bones of my spiritual frame. In every verse and prophetic story, I received nourishment and healing.

Finally, Mum sat me down for a heart-to-heart.

"What has happened to you, Ian? We're worried about you."

And this time, I filled in all the details of my journey to heaven and back.

"I saw *you,* Mum."

"What? When?"

"I was paralyzed in the back of an ambulance speeding to the Quatre Borne emergency room, and I saw—and—I *knew* that you were praying for me. Jesus answered your prayers, Mum. Here I am. I called out to God, and he rescued me!"

Mum sobbed. She recounted how God had told her that her eldest son Ian was nearly dead and that she needed to pray for him right away.

It was that same night when she was praying that I saw her face in the ambulance encouraging me to call out to God from my heart.

A tragedy had delivered her boy home as a true believer in Christ.

Dad missed the formerly cocky Ian McCormack. He enlisted Kerry to ask me for coffee and doughnuts at her mother's home. I didn't want to be rude to Rhonda…

"Kerry tells me that you had an amazing experience. You died and went to heaven?" Rhonda asked.

Rhonda's kitchen table became my first pulpit as I testified about seeing the Light of the World. It took a full Sunday afternoon, and Rhonda struggled to hold back her tears.

"I've read about this, Ian. This life after death experience has happened to other people too. I believe that you really saw Jesus! You know, Kerry is going to church tonight, and it would mean a lot to her if you went with her. She has really missed you."

I recalled the Anglican cathedral my family attended sometimes, and I shivered at the thought of going. Only once in several years had I violated the sacred space of worship—and that was to keep my promise to God after he rescued my friends and me from drowning at sea. In that Catholic Church in Mauritius, the Jesus grimacing in agony on an elevated cross wasn't remotely like the Jesus I met in heaven.

"Ian, if you feel uncomfortable at church, come right back here. We'll have coffee and a Danish together."

Rhonda's humor and kindness caught me off guard, and I relented out of simple Kiwi courtesy. I didn't expect church to strengthen my bond to Jesus—but I was dead wrong.

"Isn't this the old supermarket building?" I asked Kerry.

"It's the Hamilton Assemblies of God now."

Kerry led the way to double doors lit up with a celestial glow that I believe God designed for my critical eyes. Suddenly, I wanted to see who was inside this supermarket church. I followed Kerry down a wide aisle between rows of plain folk, most dressed in jeans and shorts. Young and old swayed to the beat of a lively band (in church!), and a symphony of worship overwhelmed my misgivings.

No pews, but chairs . . . and where are the stained-glass windows?

The last song ended—and I wondered if they were clapping for some performance I missed. Kerry found seats toward the back, and I noticed that the large, wooden cross behind the pulpit was *empty*.

The glow I had seen emanating from the church entrance now shone on the face of a man who trotted to a diminutive pulpit. I barely recall his sermon, but deep in my spiritual personhood, the message of the gospel affirmed and ignited the Light of Christ inside me.

Come unto me, all ye that labor and are heavy laden, and I will give you rest. Take my yoke upon you and learn of me; for I am meek and lowly in heart: and ye shall find rest unto your souls. For my yoke is easy, and my burden is light. (Matthew 11:28-30 KJV)

"Come to the front if you will surrender your life to Jesus . . . " the pastor said.

As I stood up, another voice raked my consciousness. *What are you doing, you fool!*

The challenge from my spiritual foe was exactly what I needed to dodge feet and gain the aisle. In the front of Kerry's supermarket church, I stood like a statue, hands sweating. I had given my heart to Jesus on an ambulance ride to the Quatre Borne hospital, but I wanted my confession of faith to resound publicly.

The pastor prayed for people beside me, and a twinge of fear fingered my shoulders.

What if these Christians find out about me? They would curse me if they knew what a wretched man I am!

But God answered my fears. The pastor grabbed my arm. I stared down at his white tennis loafers, and they stirred my memory of gazing servilely at a cab driver's feet as I begged for my life. I began to weep.

Jesus had carried me *home,* healing me from the stings of five poison-laden sea wasps! At Jesus's invitation, I had traveled to heaven and back—to my family. The comfort I felt standing with the people praying around me seemed familiar. I realized that I had experienced this same comfort when I was with Jesus. A longing to serve God seized me.

Before the service ended, one man in the congregation zeroed in, probing me for my spiritual condition. Remarkably, the dark-haired man with intense brown eyes didn't flinch when I told him that I had *seen* Jesus. Ethan was a Messianic Jew, and we had more in common than our faith. He had seen Jesus too!

Years before, Christ had appeared to Ethan when he was a cocaine dealer. The shock of watching Jesus step into his room *through* a wall terrified Ethan, and he had heeded God's warning about his eternal destiny. Jesus exited through the wall, and my new friend had immediately flushed a kilo of coke down the toilet.

Ethan gave his heart to Christ and served him at the supermarket church in Hamilton. He was also Kerry's home-group leader—and became my mentor and Bible teacher for the next few months.

Because I had died and returned to life in Mauritius, my ocean baptism at Hot Water Beach held immense significance for me. This was no Anglican sprinkling. Ethan dunked me in the same waves that had mastered me as a hedonistic surfer—my baptism was the symbol of dying to my old life and being reborn into a clean life serving Jesus.

COWS IN MY MOUNT OF OLIVES

"But when is Ian going back to work?"

My father wasn't the only one who wanted to know. No one understood my need for seclusion. Weeks passed, and I hungered to find God's will for my life. I hoped that Jesus would shine His light on a path for me to follow.

Ethan had suggested that I focus upon the New Testament. This is where I learned about the Holy Spirit, whom I had always disregarded. He had been pleading for me to submit to God—long before I became a believer.

My Church of England catechism had introduced me to a watered-down version of the Holy Ghost, and I found that many other denominations barely acknowledged the intimacy Jesus felt toward the Spirit of God. In reading the gospels and Acts of the Apostles, I discovered that the Holy "Ghost" *was* God. He was also called The Spirit of Jesus, and he held open the door of heaven for Ian McCormack.

The Holy Spirit had taken up residence in my spiritual personhood, comforting me in traumatic times and helping me express myself in prayer when I was at the end of my rope. The Holy Spirit became my prayer partner—the third person of the Godhead who traversed between the unseen world and my natural world. The Spirit always reminded me to proffer gratitude and exalt my Light Giver—Jesus Christ, the Son of God.

Home in New Zealand, my relationships with friends and family drifted in turbulent waters. It broke my heart to see Dad blinded by my spiritual enemy, Satan. I longed to lead him to Jesus and freedom, but years would pass before he opened his heart to God.

Mum—though she had experienced her own visitation by Jesus as a young woman—adhered to the Anglican culture, shunning talk about miracles. Such discussions moved her to tears.

Among my friends, too, I tried to gauge the reception before I told my story. Some sat spellbound, like my words touched something deep and hopeful. Others rejected the premise that Jesus existed at all and chalked up my death-to-life experience as extraordinary brain function induced by the jellyfish stings.

For the farmers who knew me as their supportive dairy consultant in years past, my reputation served as the underpinning for my credibility. Christian groups began asking me to share my testimony—even those with dispensational views of scripture (doctrine that miracles have ceased after the apostles died). The hunger to know that Jesus still reaches into the natural world to reveal himself through miracles transcended denominations.

As for Kerry and me, our relationship might have matured. But instead, it ended amicably as God carried us past one another like vessels driven by separate tailwinds.

God helped me answer my family's demand to "get my head out of the clouds" and land a job. My sister Sharon broached the subject at Neil's wedding. She had married a dairyman, and their farm lay in a rural community of Okoroire. This area is known for its hot springs. My main mode of transportation was my brother-in-law's motorbike at the time. When a car was unavailable, I could ride to Hamilton from Okoroire in about 90 minutes for church services.

"We need help, and you need the *yakka* [hard work], Ian."

I agreed. It was time. Somehow helping to manage and milk 360 cows appealed to me. It was solitary work, and I needed a peaceful and reflective "Mount of Olives" where I could think and pray like Jesus and his disciples did.

Sharon and Wayne opened their home and heart to me as I settled into seven-days-a-week milking routines. In the milking parlor, I occasionally slugged it out with impatience and discouragement. But at times, with cows milling about, I also laid claim to a wonderful communion with Jesus.

My friendships with Ethan and other Christians grew stronger as each of us revealed details about our conversions at home-group meetings. Some of us had been delivered from drug addictions and were healing from mental breakdowns. Others testified to personal miracles that had drawn them to Jesus. Our uncomplicated exegesis (explanation and interpretation) of scripture summoned powerful interactions with the Holy Spirit.

It was at these meetings that I opened up about my death-to-life experience, and my story caught the interest of local folk beyond our home-group . . .

The first time I shared my testimony at a local church, I nervously made my way to the pulpit. I knew the faces in the small audience. They were farmers whose crossed arms told me that the only reason they would listen to my story was out of professional courtesy for my work as a dairy consultant. Before leaving on my OE, I had counseled them on everything from milk production to pasture management. They knew me.

But did they believe me? I couldn't tell by their somber expressions, but their warm handshakes after the meeting encouraged me. What revealed their hearts to me was how many invitations I received to share my story at other meetings. Some snickered. Others wept as they remembered loved ones who had been called to heaven before them.

And never had I known such fulfillment as when I spoke about my own spiritual journey. I was a "baby" Christian, free from any denominational structure, and I naively applied my faith in Jesus (whom I had met) to problems like His disciples did. In my transition from atheist to believer, my worldview quaked as I adjusted to a new life paradigm. I was learning to "walk in the Spirit"—a continuum of awareness that I lived and worked within God's sovereign plan.

And I prayed about *everything.*

At the farm, if a cow fell sick, I prayed for its healing. Sully, one of the local dairy farmers, slipped on the wet milking parlor deck. So, I seized the occasion to pray for his healing like I read about in the Bible. I had also seen physical healings take place when pastors prayed at Hamilton AOG—but would God show up in a cow barn if a rookie Christian like me prayed?

"Can I pray for ya, mate?" I asked Sully.

"Couldn't hurt, I guess."

Kneeling on the concrete floor in my squeaky gumboots, I grasped Sully's leg and touched his back. The dairyman closed his eyes uncomfortably—due to pain (or my close physical contact). After I prayed, Sully said that he felt a warmth flow through him, and the pain faded away.

My brother-in-law, Wayne, and sister, Sharon, barely acknowledged the miracle. They were just happy that their neighbor could keep to the milking schedule.

But during my year on Sharon and Wayne's dairy, two more powerful happenings occurred that were more consequential to the future of our family.

Most of us with the McCormack bloodline are known to be overachievers, and Sharon was no exception. Being so single-minded is what makes us good at our jobs, especially farming.

Perhaps Sharon had second thoughts about inviting me to work on her dairy when she found out how single-minded her little brother was about leading her to Jesus. She made it clear that she wasn't interested in my story, or miracles at the dairy—or Jesus.

When I spoke of God's love for her, I disrupted Sharon's focus on dairy management. She avoided working alone with me until a day when several cows were tardy for their milking appointment.

"Hop on. We'll go get 'em."

Sharon hesitated but climbed onto the motorbike behind me. As I drove, God reminded me of Sully's healing when I gripped his leg and touched his back. Did physical contact somehow enrich my prayer for someone? I didn't know, but Sharon held on to me for dear life, so it certainly was worth a try...

"Lord Jesus, I stand in the gap for my sister. Save her, Lord. Cause her to choose a new direction and give her life to you."

It was a simple prayer mumbled over the staccato of an old motorbike—yet powerfully effective. A week later, my beloved sister knocked on my bedroom door to tell me she wanted to know my Savior, Jesus. Sharon became the first person I ever led to Christ.

Then, Wayne stood in the prayer crosshairs of his single-minded wife.

"Ian, Wayne won't let me put my hands on him to pray. He shrugs me off. What am I doing wrong?"

Was some oppressive spirit repulsed by Sharon's intercession?

"The next time Wayne hugs you, hold on and pray then," I suggested.

We didn't know until later that the Holy Spirit had conditioned Wayne before Sharon prayed. Wayne had heard my testimony. A cow had also been healed from going blind. These were verifying ingredients in his future decision.

It was about midnight when Wayne, agitated, came to my room one night.

"I want to become a Christian, Ian."

I couldn't have been more thrilled by God's answer to Sharon's prayer for her husband. I led him in a prayer to Jesus for forgiveness, and we noticed that Sharon stood crying at the door. Wayne raised his hands in praise to God, as I reached forward to pray for the power of the Holy Spirit to come upon him. But before I could lay my hands upon him, he unexpectedly fell onto the floor like a sack of spuds!

In minutes, my brother-in-law regained his feet and said that God had given him a vision! He had been *with* Jesus. He described pure love radiating from his Lord, whose face shone like the sun. Jesus wore a dazzling white robe...

It struck me as a little amusing, and I told Wayne, "I had to die to see Jesus, mate. You just walk into my bedroom, and there he is!"

A very close missionary friend baptized Sharon and Wayne in his swimming pool.

Leading my sister and brother-in-law to Christ marked two wonderful events that I treasure. But one final episode at my dairy Mount of Olives changed the course of my life forever. It happened at a fork in the road where my drive and ambition cried out for guidance—and the Holy Spirit pointed to The Way.

CHAPTER 7

RENDEZVOUS

White Ship

"Dad! What *was* that?"

I was ten years old, and my father and I stared at the New Zealand sky in awe. We were tracking a wild deer in a remote region outside of Rotorua. Dew clung to cobwebs spun by morning spiders, and we had tramped through a stretch of prickly brambles.

Without warning, a glowing ball of rock streaked across the clearing high above us, leaving a white tail of smoke in its wake. We stood together, a sturdy cedar and a gangly sapling, our minds imprinting a galactic father-son memory.

"A meteor," my father said reverently, close to a whisper. The meteor had singed the air above us during our hunting trip.

Now I was 27.

Nearly a year had passed working for my sister at her dairy, and I wished that God would illuminate my path with some heaven-sent signal—like a fireball.

The last cow had been milked for the day, and my McCormack restlessness blundered toward impatience, and that wasn't a good sign.

How long will I be milking cows for Sharon and Wayne, Lord? Surely, I could perform tasks more spiritual and useful to God's kingdom!

A missionary fervor filled my sails after reading two books by Don Richardson: *Peace Child* and *Lords of the Earth*. The missionaries' stories inspired me. I identified with their adventurous temperaments and their yearnings to preach the gospel to the primitive peoples in remote regions of the world. In *Peace Child*, Don and Carol Richardson unlocked a secret analogy within a treacherous tribe's mythology, and reached them for Christ.

Miraculous!

In *Lords of the Earth,* I met a man hewn from the same flint as myself, an Australian named Stan Dale. As an adventurer, soldier, and missionary, Dale found an uncomfortable niche among the missionary societies of the '60s. Dale was stubborn and obsessive about God's call to share the gospel. His rugged life had prepared him for the rigors of ministering to the cannibals of New Guinea—where he was martyred.

After Dale's death, other missionaries responded to the voice of Jesus and trekked the jungle trails to reach the demon-worshiping Yali tribe with the gospel of freedom. Dale was a trailblazer.

Was God calling *me* to be a progeny of this trailblazer? If so, how could I finance my missionary call? Most missionaries I knew were subsidized by churches. Should I go back to consulting and build up a war chest for Jesus?

As I struggled to know God's will, an "opportunity" fell into my lap. A neighbor across the road from my sister's farm approached me about converting his dry stock sheep farm to a dairy farm. He wanted to partner with me in a lucrative 200-cow milking business.

I prayed for God's blessing on my plans, poised to sign a binding contract, when Jesus stopped me dead in my tracks. I was about to plow in the wrong field...

Will you follow me? Jesus asked.

Exasperated at the question, I replied, "Lord! I *am* following you."

Will you follow me anywhere—as a pastor of a church or as a street corner preacher?

The thought of church board meetings, budgets, and humdrum pastoral routines set my teeth on edge.

"Yes, Lord," I said, "but you know that I'm not cut out to be a typical pastor. You have better candidates than me. And Lord, I've made so many mistakes..."

Do I make mistakes, Ian?

I swallowed hard. "No, Lord."

Make your choice, Ian.

I chose to tear up the blueprint for my life and follow the Creator of the Universe day by day. Shaken by this divine commission—in a milking parlor with only cows as my witness—I asked God for confirmation.

The confirmation came that evening at a home-group. It appeared that my friends were privy to my commission before I was. The theme of the evening centered upon a passage in the gospel of Mark where Jesus told his disciples to "go into all the world and preach the gospel..."

Jesus's command resonated deep in my soul, and I received this charge to his disciples as my own. A pastor and others at the home-group "sent" me out as an ambassador for Jesus. I felt like a first-century disciple. Nothing would ever be the same.

I woke the next morning at four o'clock, no closer to fulfilling the commission to go into all the world than when I milked cows the months before. My decision to quit the dairy business altogether baffled my family. Yet, I believed that God had tasked me to prepare for full-time ministry—how and where, I did not have a clue.

A priest who knew me well offered to sponsor me to become an Episcopalian clergyman, and I declined graciously. My beyond-natural experience would have conflicted with their teaching. Friends suggested that I enroll in a Bible college, but I felt bound to a shorter timetable. Instead, I enlisted in an apprenticeship program with an Assemblies of God pastor.

For months, it appeared that New Zealand might be "all the world" for Ian McCormack—until a vision of a white ship launched me in a new direction.

How does God speak to me? He speaks with the same voice I heard while lying in a hospital morgue. Is it audible? Does he speak with words? For me, the Spirit of Jesus carries meaning beyond words. Sometimes visions – or dreams or strong impressions – transcend my thoughts. I know when it's Him speaking, like when he imprinted a white ship upon my mind.

You're going to sail to other nations on a white ship, Ian.
But where do I find a white ship, Lord?
Talk to Ethan about it.

A short motorcycle ride to Ethan's house clarified my next move.

"You just caught me," Ethan said. "I've just arrived home from visiting a Youth With A Mission (YWAM) ship . . . "

"Is it white?"

Ethan nodded, and I felt an otherworldly shiver climb up my spine. "God told me to come here and ask you about it."

"Well, I have applications here for missionary training aboard the *MV Anastasis* if you're interested."

He handed me a form, and I knew that my (white) ship had come in. When I asked what *Anastasis* meant, he told me with a wry smile. "It's Greek, Ian. It means "resurrection.""

Out of a thousand applicants, only a hundred New Zealanders were accepted as trainees. I was one of them.

YWAM (YOUTH WITH A MISSION)

Youth With A Mission resurrected MV Anastasis from an Italian luxury ocean liner to a "mercy ship". Its burlwood-paneled lounge with brass and acid-etched glass doors had been converted to operating rooms. Though long in the tooth, *Anastasis* served remote regions of Asia as a floating hospital, dental clinic, and supply ship. As a first-of-its-kind hospital vessel, its cargo hold carried food, seeds, clothing, and building materials to islands without roads, bridge access, or airports.

I strode up the gangway to board the 521-foot *Anastasis* and mentally logged the location of the aging lifeboats perched on the port and starboard sides of my white ship. I banished scenes of storms and doldrums aboard the ill-fated *Galaxy* as a friendly purser led me to my cabin.

I signed up for YWAM's mandatory Disciple Training School before *Anastasis* sailed out of the harbor. After DTS classes of intense Bible study, I joined the all-volunteer staff in duties as varied as cooking, cleaning, and carpentry for maintaining *Anastasis* between ports of call.

Discipleship classes were tailored for evangelism in Third World communities, and I reveled in their overarching theme to "know God and make him known." Our shipboard faculty taught us to hear and respond to the Holy Spirit as we ministered among fearful and oppressed unbelievers.

Our YWAM founder, Loren Cunningham, had received a supernatural vision in the early '60s that changed his life. As he prayed, a map of the world appeared, and ocean waves covered the continents. He watched, enthralled, as the waves morphed into young men and women of all races bearing the gospel of Christ and caring for the physical needs of millions. In 1960, under the Holy Spirit's guidance and Cunningham's leadership, the waves transformed to reality. Cunningham started Youth With A Mission, and it grew into one of the largest mission organizations in the world. His story of small beginnings and God's miracles inspired me as I sailed with colleagues aboard the *Anastasis* to Fiji, Samoa, Tonga, New Caledonia, and other Pacific Islands.

My heart ached for impoverished families who stood in line for hours to board *Anastasis* for medical and dental support. At each harbor, my own vision to take the life-changing gospel to unreached nations grew stronger.

But within my unproven minister's heart, I had hard lessons to learn. My sense of adventure still surged alongside my Christian walk. If I believed God sanctioned an idea, nothing or no one could change my mind or direction. I served God like I surfed unfamiliar breaks – with little thought about jagged reefs beneath the waves.

My family thought that I had abandoned them (again) when I sailed away on the *Anastasis*. I tried to explain, but my sister, brother-in-law, and parents didn't understand. Sadly, I believe that I became a part of Sharon and Wayne's first test of faith as Christians.

Aboard ship, some of my YWAM brothers and sisters branded me as headstrong and mistook my self-confidence for cockiness. Living in close quarters among other believers was like mounting an untested surfboard. I struggled to keep my balance. I thrived upon independence, and loving others as God loved me didn't come naturally. I approached God with the same audacity as I did with my Christian brothers and sisters. I think that Jesus tolerated my passion to fulfill his purposes as if I was a toddler learning to communicate.

(Note: At YWAM, I met my soulmate, whom God used to tame my heart for working with her in a lifelong ministry.)

Aboard the *Anastasis,* my inner call to evangelize unreached peoples met a personal high tide. My yearning to preach in remote regions of Asia had been stuck at anchor long enough! So, I poured out my heart to YWAM administrators.

The missionary call portrayed in the books *Peace Child* and *Lords of the Earth* continued to echo in my soul. Alongside a few dedicated friends who shared my vision, I convinced our leaders that God was calling us to "Go!" and evangelize far beyond ports or harbors.

When the *Anastasis* anchored off New Zealand for restocking supplies and repair, I visited loved ones—those who felt abandoned by me in my previous voyage.

"Are you home for good, Ian?"

It was hard to explain why I was leaving again—this time for Singapore. I spent time with family at Hamilton where an overwhelming urge to revamp my plans assailed me.

Perhaps I should stay in New Zealand and return to farming. Lord? In five years, I could easily make enough money to fund my trips into Asia. Most missionaries raise money before answering their call to preach. I could support other missionaries too!

It seemed so logical, but I heard a resounding response.

No, Ian. Trust me. Buy a one-way ticket and go.

When I disembarked in Singapore, the enormity of my commitment sat heavily upon my shoulders. I had no way of supporting my vision, and I found that none of the YWAM leadership in the Asian theater of operations shared my passion to outfit a team to preach in unreached villages. I could see it in their eyes. They wondered if my "calling" amounted to a well-intentioned harebrained scheme.

But I had faced similar challenges. It was like working at the cattle stations in the Australian outback again. I would have to prove myself—and this time, I would need to count on the Holy Spirit to confirm my vision to others.

JUNGLE MISSION

Surreal to walk the streets of Singapore as a *Christian*...

Gaudy double-decker busses loaded with tourists destined for nightclubs raced past me—the names of these clubs I remembered from my own decadent sojourn.

You must see things in a new light, Ian.

I had come full circle. I wasn't telling my story to New Zealand farmers anymore, but I was sharing it with multiple races hungering for freedom from addictions and spiritual oppression. I knew their needs. Like them, during my futile search for identity, I wasted some of my own virtue here in "Instant Asia."

I had learned a lot on the *Anastasis* and now was ministering at various churches on shore, but Singapore wasn't where I believed God had called me. Under the covering of YWAM, I felt shackled to Singapore. I liberally discussed my frustrations with YWAM colleagues, using every spare moment to map out where I should begin my ministry as a jungle evangelist.

And while I fidgeted in doldrums, waiting for God to kick open a door to my future, the Holy Spirit orchestrated a rendezvous to refine my destiny. It happened as I waited impatiently in the YWAM chow line at the shore base. A young woman's brown eyes lingered upon mine—and I nearly lost my appetite.

We spoke briefly, and I planned to pursue a more in-depth conversation. What were her plans? Where did her family live? What was her calling?

I lay in my bunk that night, and questions for this Canadian beauty crowded out all other thoughts. What I received from Jesus on the matter took my breath away.

This is the woman you will marry, Ian.

Her name was Jane Stephens, and one of her prevailing prayers had been answered. She was on her way to work as a missionary in

Asia. Jane had also been asking God to provide a husband who was devoted to Jesus—a petition that remained in limbo.

Jane's church in Canada had sent her group of freshman missionaries to serve as a short-term Far East Evangelism Team (FEET). It was based in Singapore in India and parts of Indonesia. And as she firmed up travel plans, the door to my own ministry dream opened wide too.

SECOND CONTACT

The Orang Asli of Peninsular West Malaysia could have headlined the cover of *National Geographic* magazine. They wore much the same attire and ornaments as their ancestors. These were the elusive jungle nomads whose indigenous forebears in centuries past harvested elephant tusks, rhino horn, aromatic wood, turtle shells, and exotic feathers to barter with Western and Chinese traders.

I had chopped my way beyond the borders of Taman Negara National Park where a local pastor helped me locate this Orang Asli village. Suffocating trails snaked through the rainforest teaming with insects.

The Orang Asli lived as hunter-gatherers, moving their villages according to the seasons and food availability. I learned that the Orang Asli still treasured salt, sugar, clothing, and iron tools. Those whom I met were short in stature with Asiatic facial features. Wary and curious, a few carried blowguns taller than they were.

I had met some Orang Asli at the ranger station at Taman Negara during my OE. Malaysian park rangers had recruited native trackers to search for our newfound friend, Mr. Lee. (My friends and I had already rescued Mr. Lee in the Taman Negara jungle.)

Now, years later, in a dreamlike moment, I clasped hands with these elusive nomads. My interpreter offered the elders our sincere greetings, and smiles lit up their faces. My heart swelled with joy unlike any adventure I had known.

They called themselves the "Original People," and they discussed my attire as I studied them. Where were they all coming from? Children and women materialized from the forest that hemmed in acres of huts and gardens.

Some of the villagers had never seen a "white" man before, and my blond hair and blue eyes intrigued them. A few ventured close to smell me and touch my skin—reassuring the community that I was not a ghost. In time, my interpreter shared the reason I came, and they invited me inside a bamboo and bark-clad structure to eat with them. At a fire ring inside, they wanted to hear more.

Were these Original People sitting at the campfire some of the unsaved kindred that God had showed me at the ethereal tunnel in heaven? Had they been chosen and waiting for me to deliver the message of the gospel to their hungry hearts?

Over the next few weeks, I spent the days hunting, digging root crops, and repairing huts. At campfires late at night, I explained through my interpreter that the God of the Universe loved them and sent his Son Jesus to save them from the harsh demons they believed inhabited nearly every rock and insect in their jungle environment. Their animist beliefs chained them to daily terrors. I marveled as the truth of God's love pierced their most impenetrable traditions. For many, the Holy Spirit lifted the curtain of darkness forever.

Scanning my sleeping bag for reptiles, I snuggled in each night, exhausted. It struck me now as preposterous that I had considered returning to consulting or starting a dairy business.

I would have missed my destiny!

Away from civilization, memories of my death-to-life experience stirred my ambitions afresh. Missionary Hudson Taylor had struggled with his unconventional calling to China—and God blessed him with hundreds of missionaries who followed in his footsteps. My own calling glistened like the hunter's moon hanging above the silhouettes of Orang Asli huts.

I could not fathom being anywhere else but where I believed God had sovereignly planted me. Whenever I could, I traveled the Taman Negara region to meet other missionaries who trained indigenous pastors.

Often, a village church bore the stamp of Hudson Taylor's China Inland Mission (now Overseas Missionary Fellowship International). China Inland Mission had expanded to Malaysia when the communists purged Christians from the China mainland. Undeterred by the setback, CIM had reconfigured their ministry and targeted East and West Malaysia.

My first forays as a jungle evangelist to the Orang Asli served as a template for my treks into West Malaysia to minister to the Sea Dyaks, also known as the headhunters of Borneo.

After months of sharing the gospel with the nomadic Orang Asli at various villages, I returned to the YWAM base in Singapore. Scruffy-looking and weary from jungle hikes, I was also anxious to organize my next expedition. Each foray into East Malaysia over the next year earned me credibility with YWAM. Churches around Singapore invited me to give my testimony.

I described how Jesus delivered my forest friends from evil spirits—and healed their bodies, too, confirming his word as a testament to God's love. In answer to my ambition to preach the gospel to unreached people groups, God opened doors to Borneo where the Sea Dyaks of Sarawak needed to hear about Jesus.

I wasn't looking for love. I believed that I had no time to nurture a relationship—until I saw Jane standing in the chow line at the YWAM cafeteria.

BORNEO

My interpreter and guide knelt in the stern of our longboat, directing our 40-foot vessel along the main artery penetrating the isolated region of Sarawak, Borneo. The Rajang River served as a 350-mile highway for dozens of villages and a variety of ethnic groups along its banks.

A local ethnic missionary and I had driven as far as the road system allowed. We then hired Theo, an American missionary with a boat ministry, to transport us further upriver. Our quest was to find the nomadic Iban communities beyond the "civilized" territory.

More unique plants grow in four square miles of Borneo's rainforest than in the flora in all of America and Europe combined. Mammals as diverse as orangutans, sun bears, rhinos, leopards, and pigmy elephants join a vast array of rare amphibians, insects (like 9-inch scorpions), and reptiles (like the giant reticulated python).

More than 2,500 species of orchids grow under Borneo's rainforest canopy, some as tiny as a fingertip and others, like the tiger orchid, towering 25 feet. Splashes of color along the banks of the Rajang River reminded me of blushes and tones of ocean reefs in New Zealand. The exquisite flora and fauna of Sarawak was God's personal "bonus of grace" to me.

Our narrow, wedge-shaped boat, burdened with canvas-clad boxes of Bibles, struggled against the current with its puny 30-horse motor. I perched amidships with a bulky generator, planning to use it to power a VHS player. We carried copies of the Campus Crusade for Christ film *Jesus*, a biblical depiction of the life of God's Son—in the Malaysian language!

Theo docked, and the villagers welcomed us with open arms. Since the 1920s, their forebears had known the influence of the Borneo Inland Missions (an Evangelical, Charismatic denomination) founded in Malaysia by Aussie missionaries. Communities still lived a nomadic hunter-gathering lifestyle, augmented with rice and potatoes planted in clearings. A village headman spoke for the dozens of families living semi-communal lives under one roof. The bamboo and palm longhouses were erected on pilings to lift their homes above monsoon floods. Attached to a longhouse, a long veranda served as the meeting place for visitors. The village headman gave us directions to longhouses deeper in the Dayak territory.

In regions where Dyaks lived, animistic superstition bound men and women to practices rooted in headhunting and cannibalism. According to local Iban villagers, the practice of decapitating perceived enemies had ended many years ago. But my information on the matter included stories of headhunting as recent as the 1960s. The Dayak men killed to establish territory, while a more sinister motive (besides resentment over land) motivated their brutality. Though outlawed by the Sarawak government, headhunting was a crucial element in religious tradition. Skulls still hang in Iban and Dayak longhouses as part of their cultural décor.

The putter of our boat's motor momentarily calmed the racket of bird calls and bugs. As our boat ground its hull onto the gravel bar at a Dayak village, I chuckled to myself, relieved that no string of skulls hung on the belt of the shirtless headman. His greeting was friendly. Theo eased the headman's nervousness with an explanation about my visit. He scanned our boat, then my white skin and blue eyes.

Several somber Dayaks escorted us to the headman's longhouse, some 200 feet long, where women and children emerged from their apartments. Men followed, warily. Soon, the atmosphere changed to cordial welcome. A boar lay cooking on a bed of coals outside the longhouse, and they celebrated our arrival like we were princes from a faraway land.

The village shaman stood in the corner of the bamboo house. As he glared at me, it crossed my mind that our hosts might be buttering us up to sacrifice our heads to their demon gods. But I banished the thought with Jesus's name. The Dayaks' shaman represented and led the people to worship the antithesis to our loving and powerful Savior, Jesus Christ.

The Dayak belief that all objects and creatures are possessed of distinct spirits dominated the lives of the Dayak people. They believed that craftsmanship and even words were inhabited by living entities demanding worship. Shamans were regarded as frightening intermediaries.

During my death-to-life experience, I had expressed to Jesus my desire to return to my earthly life—where surfer dudes, farmers, and family awaited to hear the gospel. Never could I have imagined that I would be used by the Holy Spirit to open the Door to a community of former headhunters in Borneo.

Yet, here I sat! A jungle evangelist sharing my faith and meals with men who carried ironwood blowguns, machetes, and spears. I loved them—*every single one!*

When I broke out the VHS to play the Jesus movie, dozens of the Dayak villagers crowded close, listening and watching. At times, the Dayak shaman expressed disdain as he sensed his master losing his hold. At the end of the Jesus movie, the headman appeared serious as he spoke with elders. He turned and addressed Theo as I waited, curious.

Finally, he said, "The headman says that they have heard about this Jesus before, but the Shaman cursed the words that other missionaries delivered. Now the headman wants you to speak to the people, Ian."

The very heart of my mission was at hand.

Dayaks of all ages stood or sat on the veranda where I began to share about Jesus, the eternal God who came to earth and died a bloody death to pay for their sins. God had spoken through his word, the Bible, telling them that they no longer needed to fear the demons, whom they believed inhabited all things. They only needed to tell Jesus that they wanted to serve him forever and...

I stopped.

"What's happening, Theo?" I asked.

The Dayak elders milled about. People were weeping into their arms or speaking among themselves.

Theo had difficulty keeping composure. "They are repenting. They are confessing their bad feelings toward one another and to Jesus. They are praying, Ian."

But I haven't even given them the invitation, yet!

I turned to Theo. "Well... what should we do?"

"I guess we better *wait,* brother."

And that's what we did. For nearly an hour, we stayed out of God's way while he healed hearts of longstanding fear, malice, and grudges. Jesus had arrived, and the Dayaks knew it.

"I think we should pray for the sick, Ian," Theo said.

We filtered through the emotive gathering as he told the people of our intention. One man who had served me during our pork supper stood out from the crowd. His back appeared twisted like an ugly Borneo "strangle tree." I placed my right hand on his deformed upper spine and my left hand on his head, and I felt an inner warmth pulsating through me. At the same instant, I recalled the story of the woman with an issue of blood who touched the hem of Jesus's garment. Jesus knew when he shared his healing virtue with someone. The woman was completely healed.

In the hubbub around me, I abruptly focused on the man's head that seemed to be moving. With my eyes still closed, I ran my right hand up and down his spine—now as straight as the shaft of an arrow.

Other people were praying in languages other than Dayak that I couldn't identify, and God was touching some in other ways. Testing the soundness of my rationality for an instant, I grasped hold of the hunchback's arms and . . . this forty-something-year-old man of the forest raised his hands over his head. His deformity was gone. Unintelligible words poured from his lips, and I stood in awe, listening. I was a bystander and very comfortable to observe the Holy Spirit working without my participation.

A hush blanketed the gathering, and I looked to my interpreter for an explanation. He pointed to the headman and several elderly men standing in a tight circle. Their animated gestures worried me before Theo enlightened me.

"They're talking about the miracles," he said. "And they are coming to a decision." Theo knew that I didn't understand. "They are deciding if their Dayak community will become Christians. They trust their elders to lead them..."

But following Jesus Christ is an individual choice, isn't it? We don't do it this way back home!

I felt the "orthodoxy" rising in me.

What about the soul-winning formula that preachers used?

I wisely decided not to challenge God's way of harvesting souls.

The Dayak elders deliberated for nearly an hour—and returned with their decision. The headman spoke to Theo and nodded to me gravely. He wanted me to know…

"They will become Christians," Theo said, smiling.

The elders' decision turned the lives of their people upside down. It would be up to me to teach each family what being a follower of Jesus meant.

I opened my eyes the next morning before the hornbills and parrots started their day. As I yawned myself awake, I realized that Theo and I weren't alone in our hut. I had no idea how long the bright-eyed children and their parents had been waiting for us to stir. I had crawled into my sleeping bag exhausted and hoarse after the previous evening conversing through Theo.

"The elders have named this a holy day, Ian. Normally, they would be out digging potatoes or hunting. But today they are celebrating that God has visited their village!"

I lost track of how many Bible lessons I taught with homespun village analogies. Or how many times I cranked up the generator to show the movie *Jesus*. Or how many people I dunked in the river as a sign of their commitment to Christ. Or how many people we anointed with palm oil to receive physical healing. I also lost track of the village shaman, whose credibility had been overshadowed by God's love.

I recalled how Jesus said he only did what the Father showed him to do, and it humbled me to be present as I watched Jesus save. I visited other villages and jungle "chapels" where indigenous Sarawak pastors and missionaries had established gospel outreaches.

SOULMATE

Time flew by in my season as a jungle preacher. At the end of two years, the Holy Spirit filled my canvas to tack in a new direction—with a destination that held adventures far more unpredictable (and sometimes heart-rending) than trekking through the rainforests of Malaysia. Like slow-ripening fruit, my way of communicating the miracle of my story was maturing.

I reveled in motoring through croc-infested rivers to share the gospel and a meal of monkey flesh at a campfire with Dyak hunters. Upon returning from my jungle trips, I jubilantly told my YWAM leadership of my experiences. But due to their seeming lack of interest in establishing follow-up discipling in the remote villages of Malaysia, I felt more and more alienated.

They didn't share my vision. At the Singapore base, I learned to be more circumspect in declaring my death-to-life experience as well—not everyone believed me.

But when a door opened to tell my story, I stepped through—and held nothing back. By sharing my heavenly encounter, the Holy Spirit satisfied my hunger to share God's love with others, *like Jane Poppy Stephens.*

On the top floor of the YWAM Singapore facility one evening, I had finished speaking to a group about the ministry and miracles I witnessed in Borneo. After the meeting ended, I found Jane sitting alone. Musing prayerfully at a window, she gazed out at the dazzling sunset and Singapore neon below.

Jane immediately framed an appropriate environment for a meaningful conversation.

"So, Ian, how did you come to know Jesus?"

Out flowed my story! About a fateful night dive. About my death and return to life. About my sojourn in heaven…

Tears gathered in Jane's eyes as I described the splendor of Christ, a memory that burned brightly in my heart. I struggled to compose myself too.

YWAM is known for its rigorous moral policies, and we parted that evening as friends with an undeniable spiritual connection.

That night, Jesus spoke into my soul. *Jane Stephens is the woman you will marry.*

God didn't spell out the rest of the story. (That achieving spiritual oneness with Jane in marriage would someday determine the success or failure of my ministry.)

From the moment I met my future helpmate, God began forging my ambitions into a more useful tool for His hand. I carried an independence into my walk with Christ. I didn't recognize it, but others were overwhelmed by my intensity. Through Jane, God would shape me into a more sensitive minister and companion—a soulmate rescued from a "divided heart."

CHAPTER 8

MISSIONS ABROAD

India

(From Jane McCormack's journal of memories)

Ian had seen me at the YWAM cafeteria before our rooftop meeting. I was standing in line to fill my plate, and I noticed him too. His deep blue eyes met mine for seconds that seemed like minutes. It was as if he looked in and through me. Time seemed to stop, and I stared straight back at him. I can only say there was an exchange in the spirit, which I had never experienced before. So much so, that I went away asking myself, "What was that?"

I hadn't been seeking a relationship. I was scheduled to leave for India with the Far East Evangelizing Teams (FEET) and would be gone for months. But Ian's fleeting awareness of me in the cafeteria followed me to my quarters that night. I heard he was doing a meeting, and I wanted to go. It was beyond anything I expected. So intensely supernatural. Ian had fantastic pictures of the most amazing-looking people. Current stories of incredibly miraculous healings and so many salvations that God had done. I was profoundly impacted. This is what I longed for and why I had come!

After having the privilege of meeting Ian and hearing his life after death experience in person, I was hooked! This was one extraordinary man! Romance had little chance to blossom, but we made the most of any opportunity to hang out and chat around the base. I spent months away in India with FEET and returned to Singapore a changed woman.

Ian, too, had been away, preaching to the headhunters of Borneo. I didn't know how much he carried a flame for me on his jungle treks, but I found that I thought and talked of him often.

For me, India was a gem and a sewer—at the same time. Our team leaders led us across India from Madras, Bangalore, Varanasi, and to notorious Calcutta. We had many indigenous hosts along the way and ministered in different kinds of parks, schools, churches, and other public places.

Chaos and beauty muddled my senses. It astounded me to see whole families riding on one bike or motorbike (Dad, Mum, and kids!) Odd-looking cars, rickshaws, and crowded buses flooded the streets in a cacophony of unbearable noise.

Garbage and beggars (often children) lined the many streets. They collected newspapers for beds and food from garbage dumps. In the slums, they built "homes" from cardboard, plastic, or other materials gathered from foraging. Unless born into a wealthy caste, a middle-class family might eat and sleep together in a single room.

In India, human need overwhelmed me. Street dwellers believed that my FEET colleagues and I were rich, so they often hounded us for money. Our leaders cautioned us where it was unsafe to travel.

About 80 percent of India's population worshiped the gods of Hinduism, a caste system that categorized society into hierarchical classes. I discovered that a Hindu believed that merits acquired in past lives determined if a person was born into poverty or wealth (karma). Of their many gods, Vishnu, the preserver, and Shiva, the destroyer, were central to keeping "order in the cosmos."

At a city park amid sunflowers and orchids, a child knelt before a hole in the ground. The boy's parents watched reverently while their son offered an arrangement of flowers and food to a viper that lived inside. Hindus believe that living creatures are related to deities and must be protected. In the cities, all manner of animals roamed the streets at will. Particularly the sacred, holy cows.

Amid the chaos and sensory overload, I felt closer to God than ever before. Our missionary team showed films and performed skits that introduced Jesus, who loved everyone unconditionally, no matter the caste they were born into.

I lay in my bunk, inclined to the voices and traffic in the streets. My thoughts drifted to the cyclone that recently raged offshore. The Ganges River had flooded, killing thousands. I would never forget the sight of people standing atop buildings waiting for the murky, polluted water to recede.

The next day, FEET colleagues and I would fly back to Singapore. I needed to rest and regroup at the YWAM base. Some of our team members were suffering from typhoid fever and malaria. I had escaped these but endured another wasting travel illness.

I also explored newly-ignited feelings for an intense, unconventional missionary who seemed to be "waiting" for me back in Singapore. My fellow team members joshed me about a letter I received from the blue-eyed Kiwi. Quite aside from Ian, I was at a crossroads. Should I carry on with YWAM? Stay in Singapore? Go to the base in Hong Kong or go back to Canada? My thoughts became a prayer, and very quickly God answered. I knew I was supposed to "go back to Canada," and I knew why. My mind wandered back to Ian, and I couldn't stop thinking of him. It was then that God spoke very simply and clearly. "He's the one!"

I was confused! How could I get to know Ian McCormack if I returned to Vancouver? (These were the days before internet, phones, or any kind of social media.) It seemed impossible, but I figured, if this was truly God, it would happen. I didn't know how and I didn't know when…

So, I kept my own counsel about the matter and joined FEET flying back to Singapore.

He's the one, Jane.

God was stitching the map of my future upon my soul. I recalled two other times in my life when he seized my spiritual attention. The first while I was a teenager in a car full of kids bopping to *Highway to Hell*. Everyone was drinking, including the driver. God had interrupted my high spirits to remind me that the title of AC/DC's song described the road I traveled, *if* I didn't change my lifestyle.

Another time Jesus spoke to me while I pedaled through parts of Europe and the UK with a girlfriend on a three-month bicycle excursion. With high school in my rearview mirror, I had celebrated my 19th birthday traveling backroads, hopping trains, and camping on clifftops or country fields. We explored cities like Brussels and Cologne. We cycled down the gorgeous Rhine Valley and rode over the mountains into the Alsace of France, always finding the most exquisite little villages along the way. Almost all my ancestry came from England, which is where we chose to spend most of our time. It was even more beautiful and utterly intriguing than I had ever heard.

One morning, while lying in my little tent and savoring my freedom, God *spoke* to me. (Note: When I say that God "spoke," I mean that I heard him as distinctive thoughts that are not generated by me. Not audible, but clearly coming from outside myself. God also speaks to me through events confirming my direction and choices.)

What I heard him say was "Jane, I want you to have a good holiday. But how long can you do this for? There are people that are dying, starving, and going to hell. And you just want to play?"

I knew what he meant because there was a call deep down in my spirit. I had my plans and dreams of doing the most exciting sports and going to the most exotic places. But were those His plans? They weren't bad things, but I could feel they were all about me! On that sunny English morning, I chose to surrender my life again, on a whole new level.

What does your "will" look like, Lord? What should I do?

Who was I and how could I make a difference? I pondered many things, but this trip was coming to an end. We were returning to Canada anyway, and I felt God was telling me to get a job.

My family thought I was crazy when I told them that I wanted to be a missionary. Yet, the idea of ministering in a place like India had taken root and wouldn't die.

At high school, I had excelled scholastically and athletically. For years, people said that, "I was the one that everyone wanted to be like." Outwardly popular but inwardly very insecure. I couldn't handle rejection of any kind, and I always seemed to blame myself for whatever went wrong. I would turn myself inside out in order to be accepted. My father had been institutionalized and was physically and mentally handicapped as the result of a tragic accident when I was very young. My little brother Randy and I had grown up without a father's guidance. I was outgoing and friendly, yet I was rather shy at the same time.

No one (including me) knew that I carried childhood traumas that only God could heal.

At 19 years old, I was a vivacious young woman with a heart for God. Although He had told me that, "He would take me to many places," I really had no clue what that actually meant.

One evening, I clocked out of my job selling shoes at a high-end boutique, and I stopped by my church to attend a special service. A YWAM representative was the speaker that night, and she was powerfully anointed. Not only was I gripped by the things she was saying, but her passionate, extravagant love for Jesus inspired me. While talking after the service, she asked me what I was up to. She challenged and encouraged me to follow the call and go to Asia. Singapore is where she was based, and she gave me a brochure all about it.

I could feel that unction on the inside. Like this could be God, and I really needed to check it out. I told my friends and asked them to pray about it with me.

One of the women revealed a picture she had and wondered if it was relevant. She saw a jumble of shoes—ladies' high heels, trainers, work boots, sandals...and I gasped.

WOW, God!

I remembered the cover of the YWAM brochure. The word FEET was emblazoned across the top, as well as the verse Isaiah 52:7: "How lovely are the feet of them who bring good news . . . " The photo accompanying it was exactly what she saw. A jumble of shoes. All different styles belonging to people from all different walks of life! My friend had never seen or heard of it before, but I had my confirmation!

I spent the next couple of months preparing to go. After I quit my job and told everybody what I was doing, I discovered that the trip would cost a lot more than I had anticipated. My heart sank and devastation set in. Here I was trying to follow God, and I ended up feeling like I'd shame him instead. As I wept, I saw that He wasn't exactly falling off His throne or worried about His reputation. It was more mine that was at stake, and He loved me anyway. India still seemed to hover in the back of my mind and wouldn't go away. Subconsciously, it would come tumbling out in my speech. As the weeks rolled on, my faith grew and shook, but God came through and provided supernaturally for me. Tickets were bought. Goodbyes were said. After that, I arrived in Singapore and began school. After a whole month, exciting confirmation came. We were dividing into three teams. Of all the countries listed as mission destinations in the Far East, one team was going to India. And YWAM agreed to send me!

Ian and I had little time to socialize after I returned from India. He had returned from Malaysia, and I was bound for a final missionary trip into Indonesia. Seeing my "spiritually betrothed" again confirmed my desire to get to know Ian—but I said nothing about my "bulletin" from God that I received in India. I was going home to Canada.

CHAPTER 9

MY HIDDEN JEWEL

Uncertainty

My name, Ian, in its Gaelic form means: "God is gracious."

Jane's name, in its feminine Gaelic form means "God is gracious."

God had said that Jane and I would marry. At last, I would have a woman with whom I could share my life! We would travel together, preaching to the unreached tribes of Malaysia!

But before I shared a single syllable with Jane about my vision for our future, Jane seemed to wreck my dreams.

"Ian, God wants me to go home to Canada."

What?

My ship capsized.

This was far worse than losing my surfboard in the cave of Ulawatu. It was far, far worse than losing Mr. Lee in the Taman Negara jungle.

I prayed silently. *Lord? I'm losing the soulmate you promised me! If she goes back to Canada I may never see her again!*

Jane seemed distant, and her mind was made up.

"We can write each other, Ian."

In India, the Holy Spirit had revealed to Jane that her surfer-dude-turned-missionary *would* someday marry her. And she might have eased my confused mind by unwrapping this secret that God and she shared.

Jane left for Canada, and I flew to New Zealand for a Christmas visit before I returned to Singapore. It was my second year working with YWAM.

Jane settled into a job and renewed friendships back at her church in Vancouver—but life would never be the same for either of us. It wasn't like we had simply misread a weather forecast. We both kept our life-changing secrets from one another, unsure of the future, waiting for God to confirm his word.

Finally, I could bear it no longer. Rather than writing my usual one-liner to Jane—at the end of my monthly newsletter—I emptied my soul onto a full page.

I felt doors were closing on my treks into the Malaysia heartland, but concerning romance, a new door opened! I discovered that Jane Poppy Stephens felt the same way about me as I did about her (a whole year after we met)! We talked frankly about our feelings with one another, without revealing what God had spoken regarding a lifelong commitment.

MEANDERING COURTSHIP

I nervously sat with Fred Seaward, who was co-pastoring with his son Rick. They led a 5,000-member megachurch in Singapore. We were having lunch together in the American Club's café—a premier social and sports guild. Pastor Seaward had been born in the USA and had planted hundreds of churches throughout Asia. I had attended his church briefly and knew that Calvary Charismatic Centre adhered to a strong discipling philosophy.

"So, Ian. How did you become a Christian?" Pastor Fred asked me.

After I shared my testimony with him, he asked me what the Lord had been saying to me. I told him I had been asking the Lord to bring me to a church that had the fivefold ministries on staff in one place (Eph 4:11–16). And the Lord said that Calvary Charismatic Centre did.

Pastor Fred then replied, "When can you start?"

My heart soared. "I need to talk to YWAM first. But, I think right away, sir!"

"Good. Be in my office on Monday morning. I oversee Calvary's 100 church plantings, and I'd like you to work with me."

Pastor Seaward shook my hand confidently, perhaps informed by the Holy Spirit that the right man for the job sat before him. But I had one problem. If I wasn't on staff at YWAM, I couldn't live at the YWAM base anymore. Where would I live?

Within days, my dilemma was solved. A businessman in Singapore, who had collaborated with me in YWAM advertising, offered me a place to live for as long as I needed. Mr. Wong picked me up in his car, and his servant took our coats at his million-dollar condo.

During the months I stayed with Mr. and Mrs. Wong, I had the privilege of leading Cathy (Mrs. Wong) and Mr. Wong's father to Christ. We used the Wong's pool for a baptismal.

One morning at the Wongs' condo, God's voice resonated above all other thoughts in my busy mind.

Invite Jane to New Zealand, Ian. You are going to marry her.
This was a lot to digest...

Is it proper for a suitor to ask a potential wife to travel thousands of miles at his request? Jane may not be a spur-of-the-moment kind of woman, and she doesn't really know me.

What would Jane's family think? Shouldn't the man go to the woman?

Then God reminded me of Isaac and Rebekah's unusual love story recorded in Genesis 24. Isaac's father, Abraham, had sent his servant to find Isaac a wife. The servant had returned home with Rebekah—and the Bible describes Isaac's feelings when he married Rebekah. It states that "she became his wife, and he [Isaac] loved her..."

I reread the story in Genesis 24 and remarked to the Lord that I had no servant to send to Jane and her family—or jewels and gold to lavish upon her as proof of my love. If she accepted my invitation to New Zealand, it would be a bona fide miracle!

I asked God for a compelling confirmation to verify that I was hearing from him before I wrote Jane such an extraordinary letter. I didn't want to make a fool of myself, and I told no one about God's directive.

"I had a dream about you last night, Ian."

Cathy Wong sat down at her breakfast table. "In the dream, God asked me to give you some of my personal jewelry, so that you can give it to that Canadian girl you've been writing to. Jane's her name, isn't it?"

I stopped chewing toast.

"I will need to get it from my safety deposit box and give it to you after church tonight. Okay?"

Mr. and Mrs. Wong considered her dream to be a mandate from the Holy Spirit. Though conflicted, I accepted the gift as from God.

When I received a call the next morning from a fellow missionary with Asian Outreach, the last piece of the puzzle fell into place. Brian was a good friend. He had felt strongly that he should call me.

"I'm flying back to the States, Ian. Are you still interested in that Canadian girl, Jane? Is there anything you want me to bring her? I'm stopping off in Vancouver. Where does she go to church?"

There's your servant, Ian.

"She goes to Richmond Christian Fellowship and…"

Brian interrupted. "Oh! I know the pastor there. I'm speaking at Richmond on Sunday morning! What do you want me to do?"

"Can you check her out for me?" I said, eliciting mutual laughter. "You won't believe this, Brian, but…" I proceeded to tell my friend about the mysterious Abrahamic parable unfolding before us.

"Thanks, *servant*," I quipped.

After I hung up the phone, I anxiously prayed that my friend would give me the thumbs up after affirming Jane's character and testimony. From Mrs. Wong's gift, I supplied Brian a brooch with seven blue sapphires set between seven 22-carat-gold maple leaves—the symbol on Canada's flag. What were the odds of that!

Brian was elated when he called me again. "I took Jane out to lunch and quizzed her pastor about her too. Bro, she's one in a million. An absolute gem! Forget *you* checking *her* out. He says he wants to check you out!"

When my letter of invitation arrived in Jane's mailbox asking her to consider coming out to New Zealand for the summer, it confirmed what God had already spoken to Jane. I wasn't coming to Vancouver to meet her family. She would fly to New Zealand to spend time with mine.

Jane boarded a plane amid her family's tears. Everyone had been there to see her off – extended family and lots of friends. As she went through customs, the last thing she could hear ringing in her ears was "WHATEVER YOU DO, DON'T GET MARRIED!"

The day Jane's plane landed, I was a wreck—and what I received from God didn't make it any easier on my nerves.

Ask her to marry you, Ian.

Perhaps I heard him wrong, I thought. *But his sheep know his voice…*

Read the story again!

So, I did. Sure enough, Isaac saw Rebekah coming. He took her into his mother's tent, and they became man and wife.

What was I going to do with that?

I held a single red rose in my sweaty hand. Panic seized me as I noticed my Anglican vicar, Reverend John Ragget, approaching. He was decked out in his black suit and dog collar.

God! Surely you don't want him to marry us right here and now!

Once upon a time, he had asked me to become an Anglican priest.

That's all too weird!

As we said hello, I learned that he was just there to meet someone on the same flight from Canada.

What a relief!

We had a rather lengthy wait, but finally there she was smiling at me! We had had a 100-day "countdown" and could finally celebrate this moment with a HUGE embrace. It was WONDERFUL to see each other again! I gave her the rose and briefly introduced the reverend to Jane (who wondered why on earth I had brought my vicar!).

With all the confusion, I couldn't get out of there fast enough. I whisked Jane to my car, begging God to give me another day to gather my courage. How could this exquisite woman consider spending the rest of her life with the likes of me?

Lord, can I ask her tomorrow, please?

No such luck...

I've never been good at making small talk, but I did my best on the way to Hamilton where my parents lived. Jane gazed out the window, mesmerized by the beauty of my homeland. I rehearsed in my mind just how I would introduce Jane to my family. We pulled into my parents' driveway—knowing no one was home.

It was our summer holidays, and all my family were waiting for us at Waihi Beach, along with the rest of my dozen roses. Jane had come on an open-ended ticket for a year, so she was laden with vast amounts of luggage. The plan was to leave the excess bags in Hamilton before making the trip across to the coast.

I carried her bags into the spare room, and we sauntered into the kitchen for tea. My stomach felt the way it did when I stood on a high cliff ready to dive.

It's now or never, I thought.

"Jane, I have something serious to ask you."

We had written letters for months, spelling out our dreams. God had confirmed to each of us (privately) that our lives should be joined in marriage, though neither felt that it was time to share God's endorsement with each other.

A beautiful miracle was unfolding in Mum's kitchen. God was arranging everything…

"Jane. Will you marry me?"

My words carried the hope of new beginnings, and Jane responded carefully.

"Ian. I think so—but I need more time to be sure."

All she could hear was her family's words ringing in her ears. *Whatever you do, DON'T get MARRIED!*

She hadn't said "yes," and I was reeling. I wanted the ground to swallow me up. But this episode in Mum's kitchen broke the ice, and the awkwardness of the past few hours began to fade. My proposal set the stage for Jane's six-month sojourn getting to know my New Zealand family and me. Within two weeks, a romance bloomed into an unofficial engagement.

We finally told one another about all the things God had said and the various confirmations we'd had along the way. It was priceless to hear from Jane about how God had spoken to her in India and Canada. And it was precious for her to know that God had shown me that she would be my wife on the very first night I'd seen her.

Six months of Kiwi courtship fled past like a runaway colt. Our intimate seaside conversations gave way to include family and friends.

We began to volunteer at the Hamilton AOG, which had been my home church since I was first saved. We soon found ourselves ministering alongside the staff, and it was good to be able to work together. Unofficially engaged, we were deeply in love. And we sincerely believed that we *knew* what each of us expected of one another—but this was *before* we said our vows. God supernaturally provided us with beautiful wedding rings and flights to Canada. It was all very exciting!

After meeting me, most of Jane's protective family accepted me.

CHAPTER 10

JANE'S JOURNEY

Approval

(From Jane McCormack's journal of memories)

When Ian and I entered my father's room, he stood to his feet, shoulders back, with an air of formality. Gerald "Lance" Stephens, the former star athlete and educator, extended his left hand.

Ian shook it warmly. At 31 years old, Ian was about the same age my father was when medics pried him out of his mangled car. Dad was a PE coach and math teacher at Texas A&M before his crash. My life was upended. I was 20 months old.

From the moment my father was admitted to the ICU, Mom had devoted herself to shepherding his care. She stayed in Texas by my father's side for a full year through his painful healing and therapies. She also wrangled with bureaucracies to gain permission to transport Dad to Vancouver, Canada—where most of his treatment could be paid for under government healthcare. Mom faced an uncertain future knowing that her beloved husband would never fully recover mentally or physically.

As for me and my younger brother, Randy, we were separated, but cared for by uncles and aunts. Mom's brother, my Uncle Gordon and Auntie Evelyn Poppy, unofficially "adopted" me into their family, and I became as loved as one of his own two children. Mom's other brother Frank (together with his wife Azel) cared for Randy in just as loving a way.

It took over two years before Mom, Randy, and I were reunited as a family again under one roof. I was four years old then.

Throughout my growing-up years in Vancouver, my cherished Mom, uncles, aunts, cousins, and grandparents became irreplaceable in my life. Moved by compassion, they helped Mom acquire a house in their neighborhood. My mother landed a job as secretary of our church and rented out a room to make ends meet.

Dad was severely brain damaged and laid in a coma for more than two months. The accident left him paralyzed on his right side—but after months of therapy and assistance from a leg brace, he learned to walk again. Therapists taught Dad to write, but his penmanship never advanced past a five-year-old's scrawl. Nothing could be done to repair his lame arm and right hand. The speech part of his brain had been damaged as well. And though he lost his capacity to communicate normally, he retained his ability to shoot a basket from the free-throw line. Well, a sponge one that his playful kids would get him to throw in the hoop they held.

In Vancouver, my father lived at Riverview Hospital, a mental health institution that was a 30-minute drive from home. My family and I went to visit him every Sunday for as long as I could remember. My father never said the words, "I love you, Jane." In fact, he never even called me by name, but I know he said it *inside*. He loved me and knew who I was. Most meaningful to me as a daughter were the occasions that we shared emblems of Christ's body and blood in communion.

As a teenager, I used to go see him myself. I would sing and pray over him, and tears would stream down his face. Trapped in a ravaged body, Dad's spiritual self never ceased to be fully engaged as he waited for a beautiful emancipation.

In my father's company, I could reflect upon milestones in my life. At six years old, I committed my life to Jesus. In my teens, God set me apart for ministry. At 20, I launched out with Youth With A Mission...

Now, as I watched my father and Ian, I pondered another milestone.

Before I went to NZ, I had told Dad the story of Ian's night dive to heaven, and my father's attention had not wandered for a second. I spoke tearfully about the glory of the risen Lord that Ian had experienced. I described the waves of radiance that washed over him while standing before Jesus—and Dad grew visibly euphoric. He expressed elation by interrupting me.

"Uh huh! Uh huh!"

In his limited way, I could see that he was totally identifying. He seemed to know exactly what I was talking about, and I had never seen him so excited about anything before.

My father's accident had almost killed him, and I believe that, like Ian, he had undergone his own heavenly encounter. What and whom had my father seen amid brain surgery or lying in a coma?

It was a joy to introduce my dad to Ian, but I wasn't sure how he would act. Mom was with us, and we were all sitting around as usual. Conversation generally went back and forth around Dad, but he suddenly caught my eye. He leaned forward. Slowly and deliberately, he pointed at me. Then, he pointed at Ian...and back to me again.

"I KNOW and it's Goood," he said.

That was INCREDIBLE! My Father had just blessed our engagement!

Ian's mother and father flew from New Zealand to attend our wedding. Dad was there too, cared for by a nurse from Riverview. My mom, Helen Grace, is one of the most amazing women I know. And probably the most Faithful! She showed me what love looks like every day. Even through some of the most challenging circumstances, she went out of her way to care for and make life special for Randy and me. Never once did I hear her complain or see her look at another man. It was Mom (and God) who raised me. Despite tradition, I wanted her to have the honor of walking me down the aisle, which is exactly what she did. She then sat down with Dad, and together, they stood to give me away.

On that wonderful day, neither Ian nor I were aware of the latent anxieties impacting my life. Years later, my trauma would surface—threatening our ministry and my sanity as well.

MARRIAGE BLISS?

Lord? Did I hear you wrong?

Where did our divine romance go? My gentle Ian had disappeared, and his impatient, irritable twin ate breakfast with me each morning. No matter how hard I tried, I could not please my husband of only six months. I worked long hours doing retail sales because he didn't have a work visa. Ian spent his days stuck at home in our tiny apartment with nothing to do except make me dinner. He was unpaid, aimless, and bored.

I was accustomed to Vancouver's infamous rainy season, but the endless gray clouds penetrated Ian's soul. Canada was his adversary, preventing him from supporting his wife. Ian had committed himself to a one-year sabbatical from any kind of ministry so we could establish our own relationship, free from ministering to anyone else. It was a wonderful idea, conceived in prayer and patterned after an Old Testament concept. It was invaluable but not easy, as it highlighted the fact that ministry had become his purpose for living. And now it was gone!

We were as dissimilar in personality as iron and daffodils. Ian was nearly ten years older than me, which meant he had a lot more life experience. Months into our union, we seemed to clash over everything.

Ian imported his full-on approach to life into our relationship. I opened my heart, never expecting so many flaws to surface in him or me. He was so strong and overbearing at times. But I was stubborn.

Couldn't he see how much I loved him? Why couldn't he acknowledge *my* gifts as I did his? I was beginning to feel like I couldn't do anything right.

At home-groups in NZ before we were married, Ian tried to coax me out of my shell. He would ask me if I had a word or wanted to contribute by sharing my testimony.

I would always say "NO!"

My reluctance to speak in public surprised Ian. But I wasn't ready for the spotlight. I wasn't a seasoned minister like Ian, and this wasn't his only frustration. Comparatively, I was quite useless in the most basic things of life.

Nothing in our marriage seemed to be going right!

Is it because of me? I wondered. *Had Ian married the wrong woman?*

I reviewed and analyzed our strange courtship.

Did I mislead Ian?

In my letters, I had told him that I was discipling about five different friends at once. This was true, but my idea of what that meant was completely different than his. Ian had anticipated working shoulder-to-shoulder with me counseling, preaching, and teaching. But I was nowhere as honed or ready for public ministry. Whatever sphere of life, Ian thought it was his place to teach, correct, or try to fix me. This only intensified my insecurity. Nothing in Ian's life had prepared him for the "adventure" of nurturing a young, immature wife.

CHAPTER 11

EXPECTATIONS

Lord, Have I Made a Mistake?

Beauty. Intellect. Creativity. Devotion to God...but where was Jane's *drive?*

So much potential, yet she seldom offered two words of her own testimony to an audience.

In the beginning of our marriage, my mind soared with the promise of sharing a ministry empowered by God's Spirit. Who knew where God would send us? But Jane wasn't the woman I envisioned.

"Ian. Speaking in public like you just isn't my gift. I'm not *you!*" And then *tears!*

It melted my heart to see how hard she tried to be the wife I needed. But I mistakenly thought that I honored a mandate from Jesus that transcended emotions.

Do I still love Jane?

Yes! God had given me a miracle woman—and I was determined to be more than just a husband. I would be her mentor! To see her develop into a powerhouse for Jesus burned in my soul, and I pursued this image like I hunted a perfect wave.

But how can we reach the nations together if we can't even agree on the strength of afternoon tea? My intentions are pure, Lord—so why do I feel my ministry floundering? Why are you so distant, Jesus?

Is Canada to blame? Jane works while I stay at home. It's unnatural. You are silent, Lord. Help us. I am losing my beloved Jane. I don't know what to do—and I cannot bear this.

My marriage was heading for ruin. I packed a weight of guilt on my shoulders, knowing that my wife was unhappy—and so was I.

It was as if I traveled up the Rajang River where crocodiles drifted in turbid water. In my conversations with Jane, I could not recognize the difference between deadly crocs or harmless logs.

But the Savior had not forsaken Jane or me. Way back in NZ, before we were even officially engaged, Jesus began sketching an impression in my mind. The image developed into a vision...

I saw two clay pottery vessels being gently lowered into a white-hot furnace. Within dancing flames, the two vessels slowly melded together and emerged as a larger, golden one. This single vessel represented a oneness that Jane and I had never experienced.

Our hearts' cry had been, and was still, "Father make us ONE!" (John 17:22) This was the scripture the Lord had given me for our wedding, and I'd had it engraved into Jane's wedding ring.

Then I accepted a Holy Spirit "critique" of my spiritual life. God showed me that I suffered the consequences of serving Jesus with a "divided heart."

I balked at the allegation.

But, Lord, I have given up my whole life for you. I have sacrificed everything to follow you, Jesus! How is my heart divided?

His answer to my impassioned defense transformed my future—and saved my marriage. His revelation was every bit as compelling as my death-to-life experience.

At home in our flat, God's gentle hands peeled back my stubbornness to reach my spiritual center. There, Jesus and I evaluated my ministry. We examined my heart together, like a patient with his physician.

OBLIGATIONS OF THE HEART

When we married, my ambitions echoed long after the ceremony ended. I entered marriage with the zeal of a swimmer competing for gold.

And I knew this was also in Jane's heart. From morning to night, her life revolved around pleasing me and trying to enhance our ministry together. She savored our relationship, and perhaps I was too self-absorbed in working for the Lord to appreciate her rare and faithful love.

Living in Canada, I floundered to keep my missionary call alive and be a worthy husband. I battled impatience, frustration, and disappointment.

Who owns your heart, Ian? God questioned.

I responded, "God, please show me my heart!"

Instantly, I saw an earthenware vessel. It was like a wine casket with five taps at the bottom of it. I saw a wine-like liquid pouring into the top of the vessel, and I watched as it flowed out through the five cork taps.

I said, "Lord, what do the taps represent?"

He responded. *The taps represent people and things you've given your heart to.*

The Lord said the first tap represented my wife, Jane, who I had just given a large part.

I agreed but said to Him, "The world says if you love someone, you should give your heart to them."

Jesus answered. *How has that been going so far?*

I said, "I've never been so hurt before. I am considering taking my heart back completely from her."

Jesus then told me the second tap was my mother. He said I'd given part of my heart to her, and I was also holding part of hers. Mum's prayers had been key to my salvation. I loved her and honored her for her devotion to God. He told me I had physically left home and my mother, but I was still attached "spiritually and emotionally" to her.

I agreed.

Then, the Lord showed me the third tap was the church.

You love the body of Christ and have given another part of your heart to lay your life down and serve it. How has that been going?

I said that at times it had been quite difficult. Christians can be very needy, almost drowning whoever tries to help. I distinctly remember what it was like as a lifeguard rescuing people. The older lifeguards would warn you that a person drowning can often cling onto the lifeguard while being rescued and end up drowning the lifeguard unintentionally.

The Lord then told me that the fourth tap represented the "ministry to the lost." He told me that I had a heart to reach the unreached that would never come to church like me.

I affirmed this to be true and said it was the most fulfilling part of church ministry to me.

Next, Jesus explained that the fifth tap was my sport – surfing, fishing, diving, and golf. He reminded me that at one stage in my life, I had been married to my surfboard.

As I again looked at the vessel, I clearly saw what each tap represented.

The Lord asked me another question. *Ian, how much of your heart do I actually have?*

I said, "If you remove my wife, my mum, the church, the ministry, and my sport, then you most likely only have 10% of my heart, Lord."

What is the Greatest Commandment, Ian?

I said, "To Love the Lord thy God with All your heart, All your soul, and All your mind." (Matthew 22:37)

How much is ALL?

I replied, "Lord, 100 percent. And I'm only giving you around 10 percent. But how can I love my wife, mum, church, the lost, and sports if I don't give my heart to them?"

The Lord instantly showed me a vessel again, but this one had no cork taps in the bottom of it. Liquid poured into it, and I watched as it filled up and began to overflow.

Jesus began speaking scriptures to me. *Where your treasure is, that is where your heart will be also (Matthew 6:21). Give unto God and He will give unto you pressed down shaken together and running over (Matthew 6:38). From his inner most being will flow Rivers of living water (John 7:38). You have given your heart to your wife, your mum, the church, and the ministry, but My desire is that you give all of it to Me.*

I needed to get my heart back from them and give it to Him. He could heal my "broken heart" and allow His healing presence to fill me to overflowing.

I instantly repented of giving my heart to my wife, mum, church, and people. I gave it back to the Lord.

I prayed, "Lord, I don't want to hold anyone else's heart. I give Jane's heart and my mother's heart back to them. I don't want to carry their hearts, their pain, and their disappointments. Help them give their hearts wholly to You, Lord Jesus."

As I did this, the Lord opened my eyes to see other vessels appearing around the new vessel with no taps. It was like watching a group of champagne glasses being filled from one that was being continually filled. I caught the revelation immediately as I saw the champagne glasses closest to me change into Jane, my mother, the church, and the lost. All I needed to do was receive God's Presence. Be filled myself, and then give out of the Overflow that God was giving to me. It seemed selfish to be getting so much Love from the Lord, but then

Jesus reminded me that I could do nothing apart from Him. He told me to "Enter the Rest" and Cease Striving.

I should not try to change Jane, but from this free place in the Spirit, just Love her out of the Overflow.

It suddenly seemed so simple. A life lived with my Whole Heart in the Lord's hands. It brought such instant transformation and rest into my walk with Jesus.

I lifted my hands from the "steering wheel" of my life, and relief engulfed me. Through repentance and forgiveness, I surrendered every occupant from my heart back to Jesus—and God moved into his rightful dwelling place. Holy Spirit had shown me that this was not a one-way thing. People I'd given part of my heart to had also given me part of theirs. We depended on each other! I needed to give them back to God, who wanted to be their Lord also. If I handed over my ministry and the "things" that occupied my heart, then God would also fill those places and remove my need to perform.

I viewed my marriage responsibilities in a new light. I couldn't possibly love or meet all my wife's needs, and she couldn't begin to fulfill all mine either. God needed to be the source. He is Love in its purest sense and has no limit. It wasn't up to me to mold my beloved Jane into the wife that I believed she should be. There were other aspects as well, but God had presented me with a new series of teachings called "Who has your Heart?"

But how could I explain all this to Jane? How could I tell her that I must surrender everything and everyone I loved—including her? Would deeding my heart to Jesus finish our shaky marriage? Could I sow proper seeds for my young wife that would grow into a fruitful vineyard?

Thankfully, evaluating Jane's heart was not an "Ian-crafted" event. I shared my revelation with her, and she listened with interest. She thought it sounded great but didn't see how it applied to her. Jane already felt my rejection and wondered how she could be so bad. We understood there would be 'fires,' but surely it should have taken two years to reach this point. Not six months!

Ian voiced that he was still "committed to the relationship" but needed space to work through his own heart with God. It brought such life!

Soon after Jesus critiqued my spiritual walk, we attended a home-group meeting where I prayed for a young woman. With Jane by my side, I described my "Undivided Heart" revelation and my newfound freedom.

"I felt exhausted by obligations until I emptied my heart of every-one and everything that demanded my attention," I explained.

Jane listened but was powerless to agree. Everything I was speaking to the woman we were praying for was hitting her heart as well. Conviction set in, and on the way home, she asked me to pray with her. I had almost given up hope that she would ever get it, so I told her to "pray by herself."

Jane disappeared into our bedroom and closed the door. Time stood still. God was faithful to hear her prayer and showed her the many people who had her heart. Mom was the big one, as was the rest of her family. Then there was me, but I had been hurting her so badly that she was beginning to build walls. There were spiritual leaders and close friends also. The list went on. . .

God gave Jane her own personal revelation and said it was idolotry.

Like me, she repented and gave back the hearts of those she was carrying. She was no longer burdened by meeting their loneliness or looking to any of us for our love, advice, acceptance, or approval, before going to him. It's so freeing to be filled by the Savior and to be able to entrust Him with those that we love. Manipulation and control lose their grip, as our hearts are truly satisfied in Him.

When I opened the door to Jane's room, our eyes met. She was flooded with TRUST. Love took on a whole new meaning. With our hearts fully in God's hands, she was free to trust me as never before.

Struggling with submission, she hadn't realized this was an issue. She looked at me with new eyes, and I knew it. In a second, our Spirits joined. My heart was for her. And despite my failings, I wanted what was best for her. If I blew it, she realized God would protect her; so following my lead was not so scary. For the first time in our marriage, we became ONE HEART in the HOLY SPIRIT.

I accepted my sojourn in Canada as God's will, and He supplied a signpost in the form of a new vision. I stood on the bow of a ship with a sextant in my hand.

I'm plotting a new course for you and Jane, Ian.

God's voice was unmistakable. Within a few weeks, three church leaders in New Zealand called to offer me pastoral positions—including Hamilton Assemblies of God, my home church.

Jane and I flew to New Zealand and joined the Hamilton staff, unaware that our educational tenure would be a springboard to evangelize in nations around the world. 1990 was our year of emotional healing and discovery—a season orchestrated by God to prepare us for the following 30 years as evangelists.

Since high school, Jane had prayed for a godly husband with whom she would travel the world, and God answered her determined prayer. At 24, Jane left her shyness somewhere in rainy Vancouver. As my partner, she slogged through the trenches of spiritual warfare with me, ministering at Hamilton among a thousand parishioners. During our tenure at Hamilton, we were given oversight of 40 home-groups with an emphasis on personal discipleship and prison ministry. I received my Assemblies of God ordination at Hamilton in 1992. Jane's insightful, gentle spirit complemented the Word of God delivered by a proud and grateful husband.

The parable of the Divided Heart revolutionized our ministry and became the hallmark of our message—a beautiful, impossible paradox. By devoting our hearts to Jesus alone, we found what every married couple yearns for—oneness.

Our "chalice" of Christ's living water overflowed within our church family, and a reputation of faithfulness preceded us into fellowships all over New Zealand.

During this time, the Lord was still speaking to us about five-fold ministry and the move of the Holy Spirit. A good friend of ours asked if we would be open to hosting an American woman called Jill Austin who had a strong prophetic gift. The Lord said, "Yes." He told me to honor her as a prophet, and we would receive the prophet's reward. Wow, what a mighty woman of God! We had never seen anything like it! God opened the heavens and came down. Incredible encounters, angelic visitations, and supernatural impartations took place en masse. Jill came to the church a few times while we were there, and words cannot describe how much we learned and experienced through her ministry. Truly, heaven came to earth and people were caught up in the Spirit!

NEW MCCORMACK PARADIGM

Once again, the Lord spoke to us about going out to the nations (Mark 16:15–18). It was a wondrous, fulfilling adventure presenting thousands of people the way to receive eternal life. God had told us to go for over three years. We evangelized in Australia, UK, South Africa, Europe, and more, accepting invitations to speak at all kinds of churches, universities, schools, and conferences.

Something in me wanted to return to Mauritius. I wanted to go back to Quatre Borne Hospital to retrace my steps and show Jane the island. Because I had essentially fled for my life when leaving, I was quite nervous about going back. I didn't really want anyone to know we were going, and I didn't contact anyone there until we'd arrived. We stayed with a young South African family on the other side of the island. They kindly lent us a car, so we were able to get our own way around. It had been 12 years since that fateful night, and I wasn't sure if things would have changed by now. God had seared the experience into my mind, but it had all taken place amid traumas in the middle of the night. We'd been diving at Simone's secret spot where I had never been before, so I wondered how accurate my memory was.

We went back to the beach where I'd been dragged ashore, near Riviere Noire. Calm seas prevailed, and the "clumping" sound of a fisherman poling a wooden boat over a reef invited memories of my night dive.

Together, we wandered up the beach to the road where I figured I'd laid down and almost died. It was there that I'd first heard God's voice!

Ian, God had said, *if you close your eyes, you will never awake again.*

After strolling up the road, sure enough, there was the Caltex Station where I had begged for my life. It was incredible to see. From there, we drove towards Tamarin Bay, looking for the bungalow where I used to stay. We found what looked to be it. The very place where I confronted demons. I shivered as I remembered the spear shoved through my bedroom window and the possessed young woman trying to force her way inside. As I reminisced, we took photos and looked at everything along the way. We headed for the Tamarin Bay Hotel.

After parking the car and walking down the road, a man suddenly came towards us. He squinted, pushed his head forward, and said, "Ian! Is that you, man? What you doin' here? I not know you coming, man!"

It was Daniel, the security guard who had rung the Creole hospital and tried to save my life. Instantly, he began apologizing and recounting all the details of what he remembered of that fateful night. For Jane, that was the best! It was spontaneous, totally unsolicited, and straight from the man himself. She had always believed my story, but this was such a confirmation to her heart. It was wonderful for me to see my friend again. He no longer worked at the hotel, but he turned around and came with us to have a look. The small retaining wall he had jumped over, the car park, and the swimming pool. It was all there, just as I remembered.

We discovered that Mauritian officials seldom cast a shadow on any happening that could adversely impact tourism. It wasn't until we visited the Quatre Borne Hospital that a doctor spoke frankly about jellyfish fatalities.

"Many tourists die here," he said. "They are flown home in body bags."

Words can't describe the emotion of being back in that place. I didn't recognize any of the current staff. And I couldn't really explain my whole story, but it was amazing to be there.

"And there's the window that Simone stepped through to get me out of the hospital ward," I exclaimed to Jane, remembering how I had walked out of the hospital without ever being discharged!

We took a friend who could translate for us when we visited Simone. It was such an honor to go to his house, meet his wife, and see his children.

Baked into Simone's face were decades of tropical sun and sea. His wide grin disappeared as he recalled our night dive together.

Through our interpreter, Jane asked him, "Is there any doubt in your mind that Ian died?"

He nodded gravely. "He died. Yes..." Simone leaned closer to Jane. "They couldn't get him back. They lost him. Daniel told me. They were ready to send his body back to his country. But Ian came back!" Simone turned to me and said, "When our pole boy took you to shore, I knew you were goin' to die, Ian. Invisibles killed you."

Our hearts melted. We said our goodbyes, and Jane was beaming as we left our time with Simone. Through my Creole friends, God bolstered our personal faith.

Jesus had been my divine tour guide in heaven—an event uniquely personal. Now, showing Jane the places and people who remembered me reaffirmed my dramatic experience. My "inner journal" of events rang truer than ever.

Mauritius is beautiful. An island on the fabled Spice Road, linking the ancient trade route to India, Africa, and Europe. We had returned to this exotic island to reclaim treasure—not gold or gems but inspiration and an even deeper knowledge of what had truly taken place.

A whole year of "Ian and Jane's OE (overseas evangelizing)" was spent in the USA. We started in Florida. Then, we bought a car in Texas and drove ourselves around the country through 26 states. I spoke at Bible conferences and accepted invitations for radio and television interviews on the 700 club/TBN. It was an incredible time in America. What a privilege to meet David Wilkerson, Nicky Cruz, Freda Lindsay (Christ for the Nations), Ken Fish, Kenn Gulliksen, Jill Austin, Linda Valen, and many more. After hundreds of meetings, Jane and I agreed that we should return to New Zealand. God had said to go for three and a half years, and it was that to the day! We had celebrated Jane's 30th birthday on the "gospel road." I was almost 40. It was time to rest, listen for God's direction, and start a family.

Back in New Zealand, God had a feathered "nest" waiting for us. After 16 years of absence, the farming community rolled out the red carpet, and a fertilizer company immediately put me to work. After finding a home, beautiful Lisa was born in 1998. Just prior to that, we had met another couple that shared a similar vision. Together, we began to meet in our home with the hope of starting a five-fold church. Word got out, and many people began to come. We had rich times in the spirit and learned to wait on God corporately. Hundreds of people passed through our home over the next couple of years. For those who chose to stay, relationships went deep, and we very much enjoyed being part of the group. Michael was born on Father's Day in 2000—the same year that a familiar restlessness began churning in my soul. We could feel change was coming.

My face-to-face encounter with Jesus still shaped my every waking moment. Jane's call to missions spoke through her life too.

It was very hard to leave our home fellowship, but Jane and I felt led to resume our evangelism journey. One confirmation manifested as a vision of myself standing in a field of grain with a scythe in my hands. We understood it to be the harvest of souls and felt an excitement to go again.

God answered concerns for funding our "expedition" while a new McCormack paradigm—seeing to the needs of Lisa, two years old, and Michael, four months—challenged our faith.

We set our itinerary cautiously, according to the missionary model in Acts 1:8. Familiar lands first (Jerusalem and Judea); then reaching out beyond our borders (Samaria); then ministering in foreign nations (the uttermost parts of the earth). Doors in Australia opened wide to us.

After months of preaching in Australia, the four of us were invited to minister in a range of cultures, often sleeping in not-so-comfortable beds and eating whatever our hosts served. In hotels or homes, we accepted eccentricities and peculiarities as guests—like Jesus's disciples had done.

FALLING TO PIECES

(From Jane McCormack's journal of memories)

We returned to NZ to catch up with family, report back to our fellowship group, and carry on to the UK via Vancouver. One of the couples in our group asked if they could join us in England. They were great friends who loved ministering with us and wanted to experience what it was like "on the road." It was rather exciting because both she and I had just discovered we were pregnant with our third babies. We both had two older children who had been born close together and were already the best of mates. They would be great travelling companions!

After saying goodbye to Ian's folks, we arrived in Vancouver. What a joy to see my family again! Aside from Mom, who had come to NZ when Michael was born, we hadn't seen anyone else in years. Of course, I was pregnant, Lisa had grown, and Michael was able to celebrate his first birthday with them all. We were staying at Grandma's, and she was elated. I marveled at God's goodness and how much he cared about family.

Time came for us to go. It was always hard to say goodbye, but we were looking forward to joining our friends in London. We had a busy time ahead and weren't quite sure how it would work. It was hard enough for us to organize ourselves, let alone another whole family! God was gracious. As always, he helped us as we made our way around the UK. The guys did most of the ministry, but the rest of us were always in the meetings. The kids were little and very portable. If it was nighttime, they went dressed in pajamas. We had silent toys and sleeping bags, so they could fall asleep at the back of the church or wherever we happened to be.

I had always loved being pregnant and secretly thought I was a great mum. This was no exception. Our friends decided to go back to NZ, have their baby, and settle down again. God supplied us with a beautiful cottage where I could be stationary and a little more rested. Daddy could still go out and itinerate from there.

My internal typhoon struck when Ian, Lisa, and Michael fell ill with severe winter colds. I cared for my brood the best I could—then I caught the rampaging virus right before I was about to give birth. I felt terrible! Fear overtook me, and I went from being confident and excited to feeling completely overwhelmed. I wondered how on earth I would be able to deliver this child.

After Sarah's birth (which went amazingly well), I barely kept my seething emotions in check—until our unfortunate "family vacation."

Ian had gone to Spain and taken Lisa with him. We had a Spanish friend who had invited us to stay in their fabulous condo. She was accompanying me, Michael, and Sarah a few days later. It was a marvelous idea but proved to be way too much. I call it the "flight from hell." I was fragile. Michael didn't know our friend, and he only wanted me. I was trying to breastfeed Sarah, and my cold was getting worse. I was exhausted and started coughing my lungs out. Our friend managed to get us to her condo where I collapsed into Ian's arms an absolute mess.

EXPECTATIONS • 171

Over the next few days, it was more and more apparent to them that I had lost the plot! Unruly hormones overpowered my reality. Baseless insecurities flooded my mind. A doctor had to be called, and I needed to be sedated. Things were going from bad to worse. I was incapable of caring for the children, and it became a dire situation.

Ian managed to book a return flight for us back to England—while airline officials huddled over our fate. Authorities reluctantly allowed our exhausted family to board a plane and return to England.

In London, my anxieties intensified—unmanageable, spiteful, and enormous. I had never heard of "posttraumatic stress syndrome" before, and it wasn't until Ian checked Sarah and me into a London sanatorium that psychologists diagnosed me with hormonal imbalances that sparked my psychosis (when reality is distorted or lost).

During weeks of scheduled dietary routines, bed rest, and counseling, I confronted the insecurities that had helped to shatter my wellbeing. For years I had been walking on eggshells, trying to please Ian and everyone else. Now, the rug had been pulled out from under my feet.

My control had gone, and I needed to rest in the eye of my manic storm. Now, with three children and facing months of convalescence, Ian and I stood at a crossroads of decisions.

I spent my final days in the "Priory" mental hospital barely able to recall the erratic behavior that everyone described.

That wasn't me, was it?

After weeks of bonding time with Sarah, I felt stronger in mind and body. I hoped to resume routines as mother and wife again, but that was going to take time.

In 17 years of knowing confident, decisive Ian, I had never seen him so fragile and discouraged. Yet, somehow, he managed to encourage me. Every morning, Ian diapered, dressed, and fed Lisa and Michael before bringing them to me at the hospital. Usually, he shielded me from the vitriol he endured from a few unsympathetic church leaders when he apologized for cancelling speaking engagements.

During my whole ordeal, Ian was my "lifeguard." He held me in his arms—even when I was taking him under.

Then my father died.

CHAPTER 12

ONENESS

New Light

Jane is amazing, Lord.

I listened to my wife giving her tribute to a father whose capacity to love had not been diminished by physical and mental trauma. Like church bells, the celebration of Lance Stephens's challenging, yet inspiring life pealed among those who loved him.

At his memorial, we who knew Lance received an embrace of God's peace. His encumbered life had projected tranquility and contentment that, in death, he would enjoy forever.

At the microphone, Jane personified the hallowed phrase, "for when I am weak, then am I strong." (2 Cor. 12:10) The shock of losing her father had sapped Jane's vitality, but her Spirit-enriched voice carried through the church like a Canadian songbird.

Friends and family members regarded Jane, spellbound, as she recounted the bond she had enjoyed with her dad. This was more than a eulogy. Through Jane, we heard Jesus invite everyone present to reach out and touch the Father's love.

"Dad is healed now, able to jump high and shoot hoops again!" Jane said, her voice quavering.

Are you seeing things in a new light, Ian?

I had always connected this directive with my spiritual gifts to reach the lost. But now a shaft of God's light showed up the inner Ian again…

For weeks, the threat of losing Jane hung over me like the axe of an executioner. I felt hollowed out—emptied of Ian McCormack. Everything that was important to me was disappearing like a ghostly London mist.

I didn't want to take any speaking engagements. I felt inadequate during this troubled season—yet loving Jane back to health now shone clearly as the priority in my life. And pouring tenderness into my marriage was also reshaping me into a more compassionate and effective minister of the gospel.

Then, from one of the lowest points in my life, God resurrected hope…

Colin Dye, pastor at Kensington Temple in London, phoned me. Colin and his staff administered an international network of churches, cell groups, and para ministries. They served a congregation of ten-thousand members.

"Ian, are you available to preach at our Easter service?" Colin seemed well-acquainted with my death-to-life story.

I held my answer behind a reservoir of emotions—until the dam broke.

"I'd love to, but I can't do it…"

Colin listened, and his kindness invited me to give a full account of my struggles in caring for convalescing Jane and my children.

"So, you see, I'm in no shape to preach," I said.

The last remnants of my fearless invulnerability evaporated as I exposed my grief. I expected Colin to agree that I needed a prolonged sabbatical, but his voice rose above mine.

"It's the devil's attack on your ministry and family, Ian. I've been where you are. Don't give up! You need to tell your story on Resurrection Sunday."

God was speaking through Colin Dye, and I knew it. How could I refuse? On Easter morning, I preached to an audience of more than 5,000 people at the Royal Albert Hall, where God reignited my heart. Despite my shortcomings, God wasn't finished with me after all.

His Power is Perfected in our weakness. When we are weak He is strong. (2 Corinthians 12: 9–10)

"God sent me to tell you that death is only the beginning! The resurrected Jesus waits for you—but you must choose. Life with him or darkness for eternity."

Scores of people responded to my invitation to give their lives to Jesus Christ.

SWITZERLAND

As I sat with my wife at her father's memorial, I remembered Lance's elation when Jane related my death-to-life experience to him. We wondered, "What did he see when he was in his coma? Did he meet Jesus too?"

My testimony had bonded the three of us in a unique and powerful way. Now my father-in-law was in heaven. The brilliant light of Christ saturated Lance—and I envied him.

I glanced at Jane. Of all the adventures in my life, none seized and satisfied my soul like my faithful Jane. I loved her more than ever, and our oneness was growing more resilient as we overcame each obstacle together. We were winning the spiritual war waged against our oneness.

Jane had awakened from her nightmare, and I prayed for a peaceful harbor where we could anchor and heal. Should we settle in Canada? New Zealand? England? Australia? A wrong decision could leave our family shipwrecked. I didn't want to sail the wrong direction. Switzerland had been next on our itinerary. The pressure from most people was to "go home." But where was home? We didn't have a house anywhere. It was complicated. Wherever we went, we were going to have to have help with the children. If we settled somewhere, Ian would have to get a job. Legally, he couldn't work in Canada, and on it went…

Where do I take my family, Lord?

God's amazing choice? *Switzerland*

Doctors said it was well-known as a place of healing, and we found that to be true. The friend who coordinated our itinerary was not fazed by our situation at all. He simply said, "Come!"

We were loaned a van and given a temporary home in Switzerland—a sanctuary where we McCormacks rediscovered God's peace. The towering, snowcapped Alps became the landscape upon which we formed tranquil, unhurried family routines. Cattle, with their big bells, grazed in verdant pastures around us. The kindness of friends, like coals of a comforting fire, warmed us. A Kiwi friend volunteered to leave her husband in NZ and come serve us for a while. By helping Jane with the children, it freed Ian to follow God's call. My colleague's simple yet empowering words braced my heart like a message from a rugby captain.

"Ian, I believe in you…" he said—and he proved it by traveling with me to interpret my "night dive to heaven" narrative. We reached out to churches in the Swiss locale and neighboring Austria and Italy.

Through counseling and rest, Jane regained her physical strength and wrestled her way back to a faith deeper than ever. But it didn't come easy. I questioned everything! Did Jesus really rise from the dead? Were we deceived? Were those we'd respected in the Spirit in error? I wasn't sure anymore. When I'd had my manic episode, I was on a high. Now I was on a low, plummeting into depression over the fact it had even happened. My Kiwi friend was a great source of comfort, and she upheld me during this time. She loved, listened, and prayed whenever I needed it most.

At the end of the day, only God can truly heal, and I needed HIM to mend my broken heart. I needed HIM to rebuild me on the inside. I felt like such a failure and nobody's encouraging words could change that fact. I had blown up and brought such damage to the very ones I loved the most. Everything was overwhelming to me, and I had no idea how to change. What I couldn't escape was God's LOVE. His presence would come and warm the depths of my being. He was truly my only hope. As I dared to trust again, I found that the things that overwhelmed me so much were really just paper walls. God was enough, and he began helping me step through them. I realized I had double standards. In my pride, what I thought and said was acceptable for others wasn't good enough for me. I had to let go, be humble, forgive myself, and receive His acceptance. He LOVED me regardless.

It was God's penetrating revelation that rescued me from the grip of spiraling despair. I had asked Jesus, "What if I cannot recover from my ill health? What if a psychiatric facility becomes my home?"

And God answered, "Jane, healthy or deranged, my love for you will NEVER change."

His truth dismantled my wall of fears.

(John 8:32) You shall know the Truth and the Truth will set you FREE!
His name is JESUS!

God provided the McCormack family a loving cocoon for several months, until we healed enough to move on to Austria. Then, it was back to England where Lisa was able to start school in a lovely little historic town. We'd been in our own little bubble on the side of a mountain, so it was nice to be back in community and surrounded by lots of other young families. Non-Christians too!

For the next 18 months, some dear friends let us stay in their gorgeous 500-year-old Elizabethan manor. It was a stabilizing time where we found our feet. Ian was doing a lot of ministry and would often come home very late. He needed to sleep in, which meant I had to have help with the children. A Malaysian friend that we'd met in Singapore was God's gift for this time. She had such a servant's heart and was sensitive in every way. I was recovering more, but I was still seeking God as to what had happened. Sleep had become a problem for me. There were nights when I just had to get up to break out of whatever was plaguing my mind. I would often sing and worship, which I love to do. It would get my mind off of myself to focus on Him.

One night, I was singing an old Vineyard song.

Thank you for being just who you are,
Thank you for shining like the morning star....
Jesus oh Jesus ....
Thank you for being My bright and morning star.

Suddenly, I heard the Father sing it over me! *What? . . . You think I look like Jesus! WOW!*

How cool is that for an insecure little nobody? It was only two lines He sang, but I heard it and would never be the same again.

The owner of the house is one of God's prophets who happened to stop in the next morning. He took one look at me and said, "What's happened to you?"

"God sang over me last night," I said.

"Well, I'm not surprised," he replied. "As soon as I walked in the door, I saw Zephaniah 3:17 written above your head."

God is so good!

I started going for some counseling with a couple down on the south coast. Frustration was setting in as progress seemed quite slow. Then, one evening, the woman started praying the Lord's Prayer out loud. I stood up because the presence of the Lord became really strong. Suddenly, I was encased in light. I knew instinctively that I was standing before the Father, Son, and Holy Spirit. It was incredible. Then

Jesus showed me something that blew me away. It was a card that I had made for him in YWAM Singapore Christmas 1985. We were celebrating Jesus's birthday, so everyone was supposed to bring a gift for him.

*Oh no....*I thought. *I can't sing or dance, Lord. I'm not a performer. What can I contribute to the observance of your birth?*

The creative Jane Stephens suddenly awakened with an idea. I cut out a whole bunch of pictures and words representing all different things that I was willing to give up for the Lord. Fashion, sports, movies, sex, travel, and more. I glued them on A4 paper, forming a collage, and folded it in half to make a card. I then drew a very simple stick figure to represent me. It was just a black outline on white paper. My hands were raised, and I drew a big red heart on my chest. I cut it out and super imposed the whole figure on the front of the card. Inside, I wrote a love letter to Jesus, which I read out in front of everyone.

Now 17 years later, Jesus stood before me in this light, and he showed me my card. I couldn't believe it. I had forgotten all about it, but He hadn't. I watched Jesus trace an index finger slowly over the black outline of my form, and my profile vanished at his touch. Not only was he removing the darkness of my sin but the outline of who I thought I was. All that was left was white, and now I was standing in His light. There was no limit because nothing is impossible with him. I realized that God was erasing the traumas imbedded in my identity: some from childhood and others exposed by my postnatal ill health.

As our own children got older it became hard and harder to move them. We ended up returning to Australia before finally settling back into NZ for several years.

In 2007, Jane and I felt certain that the Holy Spirit had activated a "Macedonian call" to England, and we flew to London with one-way airline tickets. In the UK, God provided housing, schools for our children, and open hearts to the gospel message wherever I told my story.

We felt called to plant a five-fold church in London. The five-fold vision had been burning in our spirit for years. After a few months, we rented a building owned by the Moravian Church on Fetter Lane, Chelsea, known for its heritage of missionary zeal. In the 1700s, governments had blocked Moravian missionaries from sailing to Caribbean islands to preach the gospel to slaves. But some Moravians were so devoted to evangelizing the slaves that they circumnavigated the order and became slaves themselves—to share the gospel with their Caribbean brethren.

Over the years, our congregation rented another larger building in the heart of London. We called our church King's Gate.

It was a joy to minister alongside so many others. This was a team effort with a flat leadership of up to 12 others. Worship was paramount, and God was pleased to come amongst us. We regularly let members of the congregation speak, and all those in leadership took turns also. The gifts flowed. We had an "open heaven" and a "banqueting table" in the Spirit. Because there were so many others who were anointed and able to lead, Ian was free to itinerate himself. Going in and out of the country, over the next eight or so years. His highlights were in parts of Europe, especially the Eastern bloc, where he found that the deep hunger of the people would draw out the very best he had in God. All glory to Jesus!

RETURN TO MAURITIUS

I booked a flight to Mauritius without a single meeting scheduled. God had prompted me to go, and it was a joy. I emailed a few local pastors— and Jesus opened doors! By the time I landed on the island, fourteen churches had booked meetings. God's Spirit had prepared my tropical audience for my testimony.

I told my story—again and again—with the same results that I had seen among audiences from Borneo to Scotland. God confirmed the integrity of my testimony with miracles and changed lives.

Jane understood why I returned to Mauritius. I had ministered in nearly 60 countries around the globe. I had described my death-to-life experience on international broadcasts like CBN (Christian Broadcasting Network), Daystar Television, GOD TV, and TBN. The Jellyfish Man's death and return to life had even been portrayed in a Hollywood production: *The Perfect Wave*. But this was personal.

From the Quatre Borne hospital, my spirit had traveled to heaven where I received my commission from Jesus.

You must see things in a new light, Ian, he had said, and His brilliant purity had permeated the core of my being. After decades, the light in my story still penetrated the most jaded, godless adventurers.

Sadly, I learned that Daniel died of cancer. He and I had reminisced about the night he loaded me into the ambulance at the Tamarin Hotel (still standing at the time). I wanted to meet up with Simone and more of the local Creoles to video the things they could recall.

A French church member I'd met, acted as my interpreter. We visited the ministry of fisheries to see records of deaths attributed to box jellyfish—but no official would offer information about the deadly creatures. Frustrated by the fact, I talked to all kind of locals, some of whom told me they couldn't really say because the government wanted to hide the fact to protect their tourist industry.

I was in my 50s now. I marveled that I had died on the island of Mauritius and now had the privilege of showing the Way, the Truth, and the Life to my island brethren.

As much as I hated to leave, I missed Jane and our children. I couldn't wait to see them again. I always missed King's Gate as well. We so loved the people there, and I always wondered what I'd missed out on whenever I went away.

After ten years of pastoring and evangelizing in the UK, Jane and I felt the Lord tell us to leave King's Gate to take care of my mum and dad. We returned to New Zealand to settle and spend time caring for my aging parents.

My father was 90 when we celebrated his departure. After Dad's first triple-bypass surgery at the age of 55, he had awakened from sedation with flashbacks of eternal darkness.

Twenty years later, his impending second triple-bypass surgery terrified him. My mum and sister helped him secure everlasting life before his last dangerous operation. With tears of relief and peace, my father had opened his heart to Jesus.

My regimented father "vanished." He quit Freemasonry and attended the Presbyterian Church with Mum until his death. Dad and I enjoyed a new friendship in his last season of life.

Mum passed away at the age of 90, quietly in her sleep, as if tiptoeing to heaven. She never wanted to be a bother.

MISSION BRITANNIA

In my 60s and Jane's 50s, we experienced a forced sabbatical in New Zealand, due to the Covid pandemic. After it ended, we were pleased to be able to travel again. We answered invitations to minister in the UK, Germany, Australia, and on Kiwi shores as well. Jane and I have raised three wonderful children, now adults living in London.

In retrospect, my life has tumbled and plunged in a whirlwind of transformation.

God transformed my soul with a death-to-life experience.

God transformed my ministry by revealing my divided heart.

God transformed my marriage as he taught me the meaning of oneness and compassion.

One with Jane and Jesus, I try to live daily in the Glory Realm of His Love and Presence. At the same time, we're passing through this earthly realm where war rages over the destinies of individuals and families. I'm glad I can rest in knowing that HEAVEN is really our HOME!

Not everyone will believe my death-to-life testimony, but I pray that you may reflect upon my story and discover the *Resurrection and the Life* who loves you—believer and doubter alike.

Jesus assured Thomas, our exemplar of skepticism:

"Because you have seen me you have believed; blessed are those who have not seen and yet have believed." (John 20:29)

Note from the Publisher

I first met Ian in November 2019 after I flew him from his home in New Zealand to Melbourne Florida. I had been feeling a calling to find the right Christian speaker to address students in schools and churches. At that time there was an overwhelming epidemic of school shootings and suicides and God was leading me to help the kids by bringing to them a strong, loving Christian with a unique experience who could testify of God's reality and awesome love and provide them hope in an often hopeless world. Ian spoke to hundreds of people . . . adults and children and many lives were changed by God's grace. I spent over 2 weeks with Ian and we had many discussions about his life and experiences.

While spending time with Ian I was greatly motivated that we should do a more complete book about his life. There had been a short booklet on Ian written many years ago which came from a 1988 video. But I thought readers needed to know more about his encounter with God as well as his experiences that took place well after that book was written.

So, one morning I decided to just ask him about doing another book. He looked at me and said, " Chip—you can do it but I can't—God told me specifically, "Ian you have freely been given . . . you will freely give". "What that means Chip I am never to charge for my testimony and I can never personally profit from the story of my encounter with God."

So I decided to publish the book at my cost and use whatever profits for Christian ministry.

Since his experience with God Ian has lived as an itinerant minister for over 30 years-living on love offerings from churches and individuals. Also, he never accepted a single penny from the movie made about him "The Perfect Wave" released in 2014. Nor did he charge a fee for any books sold in the past (or future) or any speaking engagement or tv appearance.

Personally I found this a very powerful commitment he's kept in a time when it appears so many pastors, churches and ministries seem obsessed about money. Ian and his family have lived a very sacrificial life- another reason I feel his testimony is honest and true.

I've known Ian for almost 4 years and as a Chaplain I find nothing in this book and testimony that is not scriptural nor have I seen anything in his character that has made me question in any way his encounter with God. Quite the opposite- I find him refreshingly sincere, humble, kind and patient and truly in love with Christ who has called him out of darkness to proclaim the incredible LIGHT of God's undeserved unearned infinite LOVE.

Chaplain Chip Rohlke
President Christ is Creator Ministries
Blowing Rock, North Carolina

Contact Information

Ian is available to speak at your church or special event. You can contact him through his website at "AGlimpseofEternity.org".

The publisher Chaplain Chip Rohlke can be reached at his website ChristisCreator.com if you have questions or would like him to speak at your church or event.

May God use this book to bring you into deeper fellowship with the Creator God- the Father, Word, and Holy Spirit (1 John 5:7). He loves you and always gives us hope in a world that may seem often far from Him.

Chip